44 LESSONS FROM A LOSER

Navigating Life with Laughter, Prayer, and the Occasional Throat Punch

SONYA JONES

NBC's *The Biggest Loser* Finalist

With

CHRISTOPHER E. BURCHAM

Published by Author Academy Elite
P.O. Box 43, Powell, OH 43035
www.AuthorAcademyElite.com

Paperback ISBN-13: 978-1-64085-361-4
Hardcover ISBN-13: 978-1-64085-362-1
Library of Congress Control Number: 2018908195

Dedication

This book is dedicated to YOU, the reader.

The deepest desire of my heart is to pay forward
all that I have learned from my time on
The Biggest Loser.

As you join me on this journey, I pray that you will
not only see mountains moved in your own life, but
that you will become a mountain mover in the lives
of others.

Let's do this thing called life—*together* . . .

CONTENTS

PREFACE

Being a contestant on Season 16 of *The Biggest Loser* was a dream come true. It was one of the greatest experiences of my life. I understand the show has gotten some negative press but, for me, it was nothing short of an amazing experience!

I was always treated respectfully with dignity and kindness—and encouraged to do the right things in the right way. I felt more like part of a family than a contestant on a show, as my castmates and I were treated exceptionally well throughout our experience. It was a truly amazing journey for which I will be forever grateful.

As I was shrinking physically—I was growing emotionally, mentally, and spiritually and, for me, that's really where the rubber met the road. I started down a path to healing in all areas of my life and, both on the Ranch and off, learned a lot of lessons that I can't wait to share with you.

I want you to feel like we're two old friends sitting down together at my kitchen table and enjoying a cup of coffee while I share stories. As I unpack some of the details of my journey, my prayer is that you will be encouraged and inspired to see the beauty in every step of *your* journey through life.

Why? Because you matter! You are deeply loved—and are both stronger than you know and better than you believe.

On a lighter note, as you read, you'll notice a repeated emphasis on the number 44 . . . all throughout these 44 "lessons."

Why 44?

Well, I guess we all have our "things."

Things that inspire us, that make us stand out . . . and convince those around us that we're more than a little weird!

For me, that's my complete and total obsession with the number *44* . . .

44 was my first number in junior high sports, and served as my number for most sports and seasons thereafter. In college softball, I was #44 from my freshman through senior year. I was named All-American Player of the Year my junior year and All-American my senior year—both while wearing my beloved #44. 44 later became my number during my career playing semi-professional softball.

I'm just crazy about the number!

At this point, the number 44 has become a complete obsession with me:

- I typically wake up at 6:44 AM every morning.

- I have seen my favorite movie 44 times and will NEVER watch it all the way through again.

- I lost exactly 144 pounds on *The Biggest Loser.*

- People text me almost every day to say "It's 4:44 . . . I'm praying for you!"

- I am launching my first book in my 44th year of life.

I absolutely LOVE the number 44! In fact, the only time that I have ever regretted my lifelong love affair with this number is when I decided that there just *had* to be 44 chapters in this book! Ay yi yi!

So, if you're wondering why 44 lessons? Well, *that's* why. Because 44 is the best number in the world . . . at least to *me*. No *other* number can quite measure up.

So *may the 44th be with you!*

Oh, yeah—there's just one more thing . . .

I recently read somewhere that the vast majority of people who pick up a book and start reading it will eventually lose interest and put it aside without ever finishing.

To be honest, I can't imagine that being the case with *this* book—since I fully expect you to be so drawn into my crazy stories and zany misadventures that you'll be as reluctant as I to see our "conversation" come to an end!

But, on the outside chance that's NOT the case and something causes you to lay this book down before you reach the end, I urge you to flip to the back before you do . . .

Ordinarily, I would never encourage anyone to read the *end* of a book first and, to be honest, it will be better if you save that part for last . . . as everything in the book is carefully calibrated and designed to build up to that point.

But, truthfully, the most important word in this book is the *After*word (or Epilogue)—so if, at any point, you're tempted to abandon ship and move on to something else, please skip on over to that final section before you go.

Otherwise, you just might miss the whole point of the book. which would break my heart—because it could leave YOU the **biggest loser** of them all . . .

PROLOGUE

Beep . . . beep . . . beep . . . beep . . . beep . . .

The continuous beep of the scale has my heart pounding out of my chest as I hear host Alison Sweeney say that the only way I'm *not* about to be crowned *The Biggest Loser*'s season champion is if the last competitor, Toma, has managed to lose more than 170 pounds!

Several thoughts are running through my head.

Beep . . . beep . . . beep . . . beep . . . beep . . .

Toma has been a strong competitor—but that's a LOT of weight to lose . . .

Beep . . . beep . . . beep . . . beep . . . beep . . .

I'm the only female finalist of this entire season. I've already beaten a tremendous cast of athletes . . . I know I've GOT this!

Beep . . . beep . . . beep . . . beep . . . beep . . .

I've been the biggest loser on the show for 13 weeks in row (ever since Week Five). No one's been able to catch me—because I've done absolutely everything RIGHT! I've got this . . . right?

Beep . . . beep . . . beep . . . beep . . . beep . . .

Oh—come on, producers! This is *agony!*

I get the need to drum up and drag out the drama as long as possible—but I don't know how much longer I can stand here watching these numbers roll!

Beep . . . beep . . . beep . . . beep . . . beep . . .

I watch Toma, sweating it out there on the scale . . .

I strain to see my family and friends, shrouded in darkness, as they sit in suspense as part of the audience here in the CBS Studio in California.

Beep . . . beep . . . beep . . . beep . . . beep . . .

Finally, the scale stops—and the number is revealed . . .

There's no way he's managed to lose more than 170 pounds . . . *is* there?

Wait . . . do my eyes deceive me? Does that really say *171* pounds?!

Toma has lost **171** pounds!

Boom! The confetti is falling . . . but it's not for *me* . . .

I've LOST!

I've lost the competition.

I've lost the title of "The Biggest Loser!"

I've lost $250,000 by less than a pound!

I rush over to Toma to congratulate him—and part of me is genuinely excited for him. He's an amazing man and, if I had to lose to someone, I'd rather it be him than anyone else.

But I lost . . . *really?!*

I sure didn't see *THAT* coming!

I lost.

Maybe I really AM the biggest loser after all!

Now what?

44 LESSONS FROM A LOSER

LESSON #1

YOU ARE FEARFULLY AND WONDERFULLY MADE.

It was Monday, June 9, 2014. I was 35,000 feet in the air—winging my way from Springfield, Illinois to Los Angeles, California for casting finals of *The Biggest Loser*.

Suffice it to say, I was scared out of my mind. As a fan of the show since its inception—I knew that, if chosen for the cast, this would be the hardest thing I had ever done.

Not only would I be forced to reveal the full extent of my weight (something I was used to going to great lengths to conceal), I had to be willing to peel back the emotional layers of all that had gotten me to that point. I knew that this was typically a central part of the show and something I'd have to be prepared to tackle.

Gut-wrenching as that process can be—played out on national television for all to see—countless people have applied to be part of this show over the years. There were more than 88,000 applicants for this 16th season alone—a pretty good indicator of just how desperate people are to lose weight and get healthy; to feel better about themselves. I know; I was one of them!

After packing and saying goodbye to family and friends, I headed to the airport, an emotional wreck as I boarded the plane—not knowing whether I was leaving for five *days* . . . or five *months*.

The first leg of the trip (from Springfield to Chicago) was a quick flight which didn't allow enough time for me to get *too* "wound up"—but the long stretch between Chicago and Los Angeles was another story. I had 3½ hours for the anxiety to gnaw on me. I managed to hold it together for most of the trip but, as we neared Los Angeles, something resembling panic was starting to take over. Typically, I'm not a particularly anxious person but, in this case, the circumstances were getting the best of me.

To be honest, I was a mess of mixed emotions. There was nervousness and anxiety galore. Let's just say it: I was scared! But I was also excited! You see, I had a pretty good idea of what could potentially be in store for me IF this went well.

Finally, I realized the only way I was going to be able to deal with this would be to pray through it—which is exactly what I did!

That simple time of prayer turned the tables and set the tone for my entire adventure on *The Biggest Loser!*

I listened to my worship music and prayed—laying all of my fondest dreams and greatest fears at the feet of Jesus, asking *Him* to guide me. All of a sudden, sitting there (in seat 22B), I had a time of personal worship as powerful as any I've ever experienced in church . . . and I have experienced many of them!

As the plane began its descent, I quietly asked the Lord to speak to my heart . . . and He *did!*

In that moment, I sensed Him say to my spirit that this entire *Biggest Loser* experience was going to be my very own personal journey . . . to believing (for the first time ever) that I, Sonya Jones, am "fearfully and wonderfully made!"

I recognized this unusual phrase from Psalm 139:14, often rendered by contemporary Bible translations as "remarkably and wonderfully complex." I guess, sometimes, the Lord still speaks in "King James" English—because I clearly sensed Him saying to me: "Sonya, you are fearfully and wonderfully made!"

Wait a minute.

What?

Fearfully and wonderfully made? Me???

Yeah . . . riiiiigghhhttt!

You see, I really DID believe that . . . for *other* people.

I could hold a newborn and believe that baby was fearfully and wonderfully made. When I looked at trainers Jessie Pavelka and Dolvett Quince, I had no trouble believing (and reminding the Lord, just in case He'd forgotten): "Dear God, they ARE fearfully and wonderfully made! Hallelujah!"

*Biggest Loser trainers Jessie Pavelka and Dolvett Quince —
"fearfully and wonderfully made" indeed!*

But *ME?*

At 283 pounds?!

Come on! Really, Lord? You've gotta be kidding me!

See, most people had no idea how much I struggled with who I was *physically*.

I **hated** how my body looked. I had never felt pretty, attractive, or desirable in any way. I felt many ways throughout my life, but certainly not fearfully and wonderfully made!

I don't think so. Nice try . . . but not *me*.

Ordinarily, I'm pretty good at taking God at His Word and believing what He says—but I just couldn't take hold of this particular truth for myself.

I hated who I was *physically* and, though it didn't affect *God's* love for me . . . it DID affect *my* love for me.

But in that moment, sitting there on the plane, I suddenly knew that I was going to emerge from casting finals and make it onto the show. I also knew that I was going to be there for the long haul . . . all the way to the *end!*

However, it wasn't until months later—after that whole long, crazy, incredible ride was over—that I realized there had been an even deeper and more profoundly life-changing message in what the Lord said to me on the plane that day.

Jeni, my dearest friend of two decades, pointed out to me that God spoke those words to me about being "fearfully and wonderfully made" . . . while I was on the plane going *TO* Los Angeles!

He didn't speak those words to me *AFTER* I had lost the weight!

His love for me was *strongest* when I was feeling *lowest* . . . at my very *highest* (weight)! Maybe you've heard of the famous devotional book, *My Utmost for His Highest*? Well, He gave *His* utmost . . . for *my* highest!

I didn't have to fix myself before God would love me!

He loved me when I felt like I was at my worst!

God's love for me didn't grow as I shrunk!

His love was always there; I just had to believe it for myself.

We all have a lot of yuck in our lives.

Some of it's yuck we never tell anyone about. We're too embarrassed or feel like it's too much for people to handle.

Like I said, most people never would have guessed that I felt so negatively about *myself* . . . but I did.

Maybe you don't struggle with self-image . . . then again, maybe you do!

Maybe your struggle is with anger or gossip. You may struggle with alcoholism or any number of other addictions.

Maybe you just flat-out struggle with *life!* We all struggle with something.

The important thing is to know that you're not alone.

Whatever you're struggling with . . . God's love is there for YOU!

His love is lasting and real . . . because it's completely unconditional!

You don't have to "pretty yourself up" for Him to love you.

He already *does* love you!

Just come to Him, bruised and broken as you are.

Trust Him. He'll put all the pieces together.

May you always rest assured that you serve a God who has knit you together in your mother's womb and that *you ARE . . . fearfully and wonderfully made* . . . even if you've lived a lifetime of believing otherwise.

LESSON #2

WORDS HAVE THE POWER OF LIFE AND DEATH.

Ughh . . . junior high! You remember those days, right?

Trying not to get beaten up or shoved into a locker . . .

Trying to do everything possible to avoid having to get butt-naked and shower with everyone else after PE . . .

Whoever designed those communal showers should be throat-punched, hung from their toes, and beaten with a large stick!

For me, junior high was a very TRYING time . . .

TRYING to make sure I didn't get stuck square dancing with the yucky boy who would invariably sneeze into his left hand right before the do-si-freakin-do . . .

TRYING to tame the horrendous cowlick that was smack dab in the middle of my head (it took me years to get that sucker figured out)!

Junior high is brutal! Kids can be really mean!

It was in junior high—one fateful day that I remember like it was yesterday—when my life changed forever . . .

I had just gotten my food tray from the hot lunch line in the cafeteria. It was my favorite lunch day of the month: SQUARE PIZZA (with imitation pepperoni bits)! Mmm mmm! You remember, right? That stuff was like manna from Heaven! I made sure I got a *second* piece as I sat down at a table and eagerly began my feast.

I'd no sooner started to chow down than I caught the eye of a particular boy—and not in a *good* way!

He was in the eighth grade—cute, popular, athletic . . . and WAAYY out of my league! Ordinarily, I'd have been thrilled to have him notice me—but NOT this day, not in this way . . .

He suddenly walked over to me, pointed, and said as loudly as he could: "Hey, you're FAT!"

It caught me completely off-guard, especially since we'd had no prior communication! I could feel my face flush with embarrassment, but I quickly recovered enough to do what any delicate little junior high girl in that situation would do . . .

In that moment, I stood up, punched him dead in the face, and walked away! (I told you I was delicate.)

I laughed it off, acting like his words didn't affect me at all! Even at *that* age, I knew enough not to let him see how I'd been hurt. But, in truth, his words cut me far more deeply than I could admit—even to myself.

In fact, those words quickly began to define me. It's like, until that moment, I'd never even realized I was overweight . . . until he *told* me I was. But, from that moment on, everything changed—as I instantly grew to hate who I was . . .

> *I hated changing in the locker rooms . . .*

> *I hated showering in PE . . .*

> *I changed in a locked bathroom at sleepovers . . .*

> *No matter what I wore, I never felt pretty or cute . . .*

I felt only fat, ugly, and gross—and would for the next 27 years!

As I got older, and increasingly compared myself to others who seemed so much more attractive, my self-esteem spiraled lower and lower. I never felt worthy of love (to say nothing of a romantic relationship)—all because of those terrible words that had been spoken to me that day . . . and, to be honest, the power that I *GAVE* those words!

I pray that, unlike me, you won't give ANYONE the power to change the course of your life simply because of something they've said. You don't have to give them that kind of control!

On the other hand, I urge you to use your own words wisely!

Proverbs 18:21 reveals that "the tongue has the power of *life* . . . and *death!*"

It cuts both ways.

Your words will be either a blessing or a curse.

Your tongue has the power to *make* OR *break* people—so PLEASE use your words to add blessing and value to the lives of those around you!

God's Word charges us to "encourage one another and build each other up" (I Thessalonians 5:11).

Encourage. Build up. Speak life.

Words have the power of life and death—so use your words . . . wisely and well!

LESSON #3

COMMUNICATION IS KEY.

Having emphasized the need to be careful in what you SAY to *others*, I should probably mention the importance of being careful to HEAR exactly what they're saying to *you!*

When studying education, I spent a lot of time working to build my communication skills but, in hindsight, probably should have spent a little more time working on my effectiveness in *receiving* communication . . . especially when working with children!

You just never know what's going to come out of their little mouths!

I remember one particular day when I had my second-grade class lined up by the fence on the soccer field. I was just starting to give instructions for the day's drill, when I began to hear a lot of "oohs" and "ahhs" . . .

I was accustomed to their admiration, of course—but was trying to figure out what I'd done to deserve such kudos on this occasion . . . when I spotted a beautiful little tabby-colored cat playing around my feet, much to the children's delight!

Quickly doing the math (Kids kicking balls + Cat on the ground = A really bad idea), I moved the cat to safety just outside the fence line and forgot all about it.

The next morning, I was back out on that same field— this time with a group of *kindergartners* . . .

Dutifully marching them across that five-acre field (like a mother duck with her little ducklings), I began carefully explaining exactly what we were going to do.

Just as I was mid-sentence, one little girl politely raised her hand to ask a question.

Thinking she had a question about the game, I broke out into a cold sweat (and immediately began praying) as she blurted out: "Esscusssee me, Toach—is dat your titty?"

Dear Lord Jesus, I thought, *I sure hope not—because I really like this job, and if one of those suckers has somehow fallen out, I'm in BIG trouble!*

Looking down to make sure nothing was hanging out of my shirt, I was enormously relieved to find that sweet tabby again at my feet!

Trying to be helpful, I offered a word of clarification.

"Sweetheart," I said, "that's a *tat* . . . not a *titty!*"

The job of a kindergarten PE teacher can be a lot like herding tats, I mean *cats!*

Unless you're extremely specific in your instructions, you have absolutely no hope of achieving the desired result!

I loved those kids but there were days when, to be honest, I think I would rather have slid down a razor blade into a pool of salt water than take those kindergartners on—but hey, if this was my cross to bear . . .

One day they had just about worn me out but, thankfully, the end of class was finally upon us! Preparing to exit the gym, I told them all to stand on the purple line—not realizing that there were *multiple* purple lines in the gymnasium; and, of course, each kid landed on a different one! So much for lining up single file!

Little did I know that I was about to have yet another memorable encounter with that delightful little girl with the charmingly distinctive speech!

I noticed her staring at me and realized that, for some reason, she was trying to size me up. Still, I could never have anticipated the words that were about to spring from that precious little mouth . . .

"Toach," she said, "I have a twestion for you. I was just tind of wondering . . . tould you please tell me, umm . . . are you a *boy* or a *durl?*"

No, she did NOT just ask me that!

I confess that I rolled my eyes (at a 5-year-old!) as I put all my communication skills to work in assuring her that (my short haircut and deep voice notwithstanding) I was, indeed, a *"durl"*!

In all my (mis)communications, I've tried to remember what one of my professors said to me as I left his class for the last time.

"Sonya," he said, "as you walk through that door and go out there to impact the lives of countless students, you won't determine whether or not to BE a role model. That's not up to you. The only thing you'll determine is what *type* of role model you're going to be!"

When I wanted to throat-punch a well-meaning little girl innocently calling my gender into question, his wise words came to mind, kept me in check, and enabled me to respond with a warm hug and a soft answer instead!

Understanding is important—and good ***communication is key;*** its impact monumental!

LESSON #4

THINGS ARE NOT ALWAYS AS THEY APPEAR.

Cancun, Mexico is one of my favorite spots in the world. With a direct flight, I can be dipping my pudgy little toes into the ocean on its beautiful white, sandy beaches before lunch! I often stand there thinking, "Surely Heaven must look a lot like this!"

On a typical trip to Cancun, I'm up before the sun—watching, with my Bible and journal in hand, as God paints His morning masterpiece.

Once I've had my quiet time, I'll typically head on up the beach for a morning run. In the old days (pre-*Biggest Loser*), it was only a "walk" because, in a swimsuit . . . well, let's just say there are some things you can't UN-see. So I *walked* . . .

One particularly beautiful morning, I started up the beach—wondering how anyone could take in such a captivating sunrise and doubt the existence of God!

I was still marveling at His incredible handiwork when something on the beach caught my eye. Mostly covered in sand, it appeared to be both clear . . . and clearly *moving!*

Realizing that I had stumbled upon a dying jellyfish that had washed ashore and was struggling to breathe, I (hopelessly devoted animal lover that I am) immediately felt the irresistible need to intervene!

Though I could see only the very top of the little creature, it was clearly fighting for every breath. I knew that I had to act quickly, but was fearful of being stung—so I stood back for a moment, carefully devising a plan to help this little guy stay alive.

Finally, I decided to get down on my hands and knees, and spent about 15 minutes building a huge wall of sand around it so that I wouldn't have to touch it with my bare hands—but could safely move it back into the ocean!

It was still only 6 AM, but I was sweating like a dieting girl in a donut shop—as all 283 pounds of me struggled to push this stranded jellyfish back into the sea!

I thought I would never get there! I was dripping with sweat; my eyes were burning; my mouth was parched and dry and full of sand. (This was a *Biggest Loser* workout before I even knew what that was!)

With my last ounce of strength, in a desperate last-ditch effort, I gave one final push—so hard that my hand slipped and landed directly on top of that jellyfish!

NOOO!!! I braced myself, waiting for the excruciating pain of the sting to begin radiating into my hand, up my arm, and all throughout the *rest* of my body.

But nothing happened.

Clearly, the adrenaline was blocking the pain that should have been crippling by now!

Besides, I'd evidently waited too long and hadn't managed to get my little friend back to the water in time. Bless his little heart.

I struggled to maintain my composure as I looked down through my hot tears . . . only to realize that my hand was resting . . . NOT on the back of a stranded *jellyfish* . . . but a shredded Ziploc *baggie!*

That's right—a ZIPLOC BAGGIE!

I'd just spent the last 15 minutes of my life (that I could never get back) desperately trying to save the life of a Ziploc baggie!

The lesson here?

Things are not always as they appear—so you might want to investigate before going "all-in" to help!

LESSON #5

LOOK CLOSELY!
(IT'LL SAVE YOU A LOT OF TIME
& ENERGY LATER.)

One afternoon, I could put it off no longer.

After hauling things around for weeks, my car was such a mess that I simply HAD to get it cleaned up!

I spent all afternoon on the job. I vacuumed; I scrubbed; I used Armor All and Windex and even added an air freshener!

I just love the feel (and smell) of a nice, clean car!

Driving home that evening, I slammed on the brakes to bring my newly-clean car to a screeching halt as a yellow lab darted in front!

Had I hit that dog (as an incorrigible animal lover who's all about saving any and every animal possible – think jellyfish/Ziploc baggie), I'd have needed counseling for years to come!

I mean, animal movies are typically the only ones that make me cry, but I could have cleared entire theaters with my wailing during showings of *Marley & Me* or *My Dog Skip!* I'm a certifiable animal lover who was thankful beyond words that I hadn't just ended the life of this beautiful golden lab!

Recognizing the dog as my neighbors' Maya, I immediately pulled over to save the day (and *her*)!

Unfortunately, she proved to be a reluctant rescue—as I had to chase her for blocks before finally managing to capture her. Grabbing her by the collar, I pulled her from a mud puddle and walked her back to my car—realizing, to my dismay, that her undercarriage and paws were covered in mud.

I tried not to think about the fact that I had just spent the entire day cleaning and detailing my car—as I popped open the hatch and shoved her (muddy paws and all) into the back hatch! I was NOT going to be responsible for my neighbors losing their beloved family pet!

After spending *more* time cleaning the dog (and my car) back up to some reasonably presentable appearance, I called my neighbors to let them know that I had their pet. There was only one slight problem: so did *they!* They assured me that the dog was right there in their living room!

Never having heard of an animal capable of being in two places at once, I scrutinized Maya the Wonder Dog's collar . . . only to find it inscribed with the name "Bullet"—followed by a phone number I'd never seen before in my life!

After sheepishly picking up the phone once again—this time to call the dog's real owner—I loaded the imposter back into my car and drove to a house about a mile from where I'd first encountered the confused canine.

As I opened the hatch and watched Bullet run happily into the arms of a very relieved owner, I suddenly spotted a very conspicuous part (*two* of them actually) that would have clearly identified "Maya" as *male* a whole lot earlier in the process . . . had I only been paying closer attention! I'd chased that mangy mutt for blocks—never noticing that SHE was a *HE!*

If you **look closely** and inspect things well . . . *it will* indeed *save you a lot of time and energy later* on!

LESSON #6

WHEN PEOPLE WANT TO HELP YOU . . .
LET THEM!

Traumatized, party of one? Traumatized?

HERE! I'm right here!!!

It was July 10, 2013.

The Day of the Turtle.

Anyone who knows me will tell you that I'm a person who needs help.

Wait a second—that's not what I meant to say.

I mean, I DO *need* help (God knows I do) . . . but what I *meant* to say is that I'm a person who really likes *TO* help!

I love helping others. Maybe that's because I know how often I myself have *needed* help.

Whatever the reason, I just love to help! I help support missionaries all over the world. I help feed the homeless. I help out in more volunteer organizations than I can count. Helping is just part of my DNA; it's just who I am.

Animal, vegetable, or mineral: I'll help it if I can— whether it *wants* my help or not!

But I'm getting ahead of my story . . .

It was a hot July day, and I was headed to an athletic practice at the school where I coached. Intent on getting to practice before the athlete that I was meeting, I was cruising down one of the busiest highways in town at 65 mph or so (only *slightly* above the speed limit) when, all of a sudden, something right out in the middle of the road caught my eye.

What IS that?!

Whatever it is—it's huge . . . and it's MOVING!

As I got closer to the Mystery Mass, I realized to my astonishment that it was a ginormous *turtle,* of all things!

Now, I'd seen turtles before—obviously. Cute little box turtles you could hold in the palm of your hand—but nothing like *this!* You could have put a saddle on this thing and made a little "mad money" charging kids to ride him!

Actually, that may be a slight exaggeration . . . but you get the idea. This thing was HUGE . . . probably at least 15 inches long!

He had my attention anyway—and somehow, as I went whizzing past him—our eyes locked! Well, it was all over then! In that magic moment, his beautiful but desperate eyes spoke volumes, and I knew exactly what they were saying: he needed my help! (Besides, he was really *cute* . . .)

As I mentioned, however, this was a VERY busy highway, so it was clear that I had to act quickly or my new friend Tommy the Turtle would be turtle *wax!* If I didn't act fast, he was going to DIE!

Immediately pulling off to the side of the road, I put my hazard lights on and, as soon as a sudden onslaught of traffic had passed, sprang into action and dashed out into the highway to try and draw my new friend out of his shell, so to speak.

Sonya Jones, Turtle Savior to the rescue . . .

As I came closer, he looked up at me and, with a single glance, conveyed a message I will never forget . . . and could not ignore!

"Sonya" (he was calling my name)—help me! I'm *lost*. I somehow got all turned around, and now I'm stuck out here in the middle of this busy highway! I'm going just as fast as my little legs will carry me but I am, after all, a *turtle* soooo . . . ."

I leapt into action as my heart responded, saying: "I get it, Tommy; I get it. Fate has brought us together for a reason, so have no fear; SJ is here! Just hang on, my friend; Sonya is here to *help!*"

Bending down to pick Tommy up with both hands, I was shocked when my beloved suddenly turned around and snapped at me! The rascal actually tried to *bite* me!

"Really, Tommy? Seriously?! After all we've been through together, *this* is how you treat me?"

Turning all the way around, he extended his legs to stand as tall as possible, puffing himself up as he walked toward me . . . *hissing* the entire time!

The little ingrate was *hissing* at me! How rude!

He kept coming; in fact, he was practically *charging* me by this time, hissing the whole way . . . like he was challenging me to a duel or something—right here out in the middle of a busy highway!

With vehicles fast approaching, I hustled back to my car just as quickly as I could; but as soon as I was safely back inside, I cast a glance back in Tommy's direction.

He looked like some terrifying combination of both mean . . . and *mad!*

I'm thinking *"I'm* the one who should be mad"; but, from the safety of my driver's seat, I rolled down my window and tried to explain that he needn't be so mean. I was only trying to help him across the road to save his miserable little life!

"Look, Tommy," I said, "If you want to have friends, you have to be *friendly!*"

He seemed thoroughly unimpressed as he continued hissing and snapping at me, completely oblivious to the fact that it was no small miracle he'd thus far been able to avoid being hit by all the traffic!

Afraid it was only a matter of time, however, I cast a frantic glance in my backseat, searching for something I might use to help the sorry thing!

After all, once I had a moment to think about it, I realized that he was only acting out of fear . . . but, deep down, probably loved me just as much as I did him. He was just scared. Shoot—*I'd* be scared too! So how could I *not* extend the poor little fella some grace and mercy here?!

Rummaging through my backseat, I finally found some hula hoops and pool noodles. (Hey, don't judge me; we were in the middle of my church's Vacation Bible School at the time!)

"These oughta work," I thought—as I rushed back out, boldly risking my life once again to rescue my friend.

And, once again, the minute I got close, he started to lunge and snap, nearly snagging my pool noodle in the process! Are you kidding me?!

Now *I'm* mad! Here I am—out in the middle of a busy highway, yelling at a sadistic turtle to "BE NICE!"

About that time, Tommy actually started *hopping* as he hissed! That's when I realized: he wasn't *scared!* He was *possessed!* This slimy spawn of Satan was trying to end *his* life AND *mine!*

It was then that it dawned on me how ridiculous this whole scene must have looked! Here I was . . . in the middle of a busy highway with a blue hula hoop and yellow pool noodle trying to scoot this blasted turtle off the road to the safety of a grassy area. To any puzzled passerby, it must have looked like I was trying to get my pet turtle to jump through the hoop! *Grrrr*—stupid, satanic turtle!

Trying once more to push him toward the safety of the grass, I couldn't believe my eyes when he turned on me, snapping and hissing, yet again!

I knew he meant business this time because he was actually *running* at me. Now, even before *The Biggest Loser,* I could outrun a *turtle*—but he was really charging, "full steam ahead"—so I wasn't wasting any time in getting away from him!

I did the only thing I could and ran back to jump in my car, yelling at the turtle the whole time!

"Look, Tommy," I said, "you're going to DIE! And whose fault will that be? Not mine, Tommy; not mine! I'm just trying to help you, and you don't want to do anything but BITE me! That's partly what's wrong with turtles these days . . . always trying to bite the hand that feeds 'em!" Ugh!

Apparently, my motivational talk failed to move Tommy—as he continued coming toward me—hopping, snapping and hissing all at the same time!

All this because I didn't want to see the awful thing killed! My heart of gold simply wouldn't let me drive away!

Determined to make one final attempt, I grabbed a metal pole from the backseat of my car, hoping I could use it to scoot the turtle to the side of the road. At least it was long enough that I could keep a safe distance away from the little beast; I was hoping that, even if he bit the pole, I could still drag Chucky the Devil Turtle out of harm's way!

As I reached around into the backseat to grab the metal pole, it happened. I heard a sickening *SCREECH, SPLAT, CRUNCH, CRACKLE, SNAP!!!!*

I was afraid to look . . .

Was that . . . ? Did he . . . ? Is he . . . ?

You guessed it!

"Mr. Reptile, meet Mr. Rubber Tire!"

I sat there in complete and utter disbelief! My sweet, precious turtle was gone! All that was left in the wake of a blue Ford Explorer were pieces of shattered shell, with red blood and gray slime splattered and smeared all over the road!

My eyes began to fill with tears. *Poor Tommy!*

I'd had such plans for our future together!

Sure, we had some trust and anger issues but, with the proper counseling, we could overcome anything together.

I looked up from Tommy's crushed and crumpled corpse to see this horrible man backing up toward me.

Getting out of his offending car, he came to my window.

"What WAS that?!" he asked.

Struggling to speak in my sorrow and shock, I finally managed. "It was my turtle!"

"Ma'am," he said, "I am so sorry! I tried to swerve, but there was a car in the other lane—and I just couldn't get over in time!"

I just shrugged my shoulders. "It's not your fault," I said. "There's nothing you could have done."

As he walked off, I bade my old friend one fond and final farewell. "Goodbye, sweet friend" was all I could muster.

Driving off, I glanced back in my rearview mirror just in time to see a white pickup truck hit my late friend yet again, this time thrusting what was left of him into the grassy area . . . *where I'd tried to get him all along!*

Stupid turtle. But . . . he was MY stupid turtle.

Today's lesson from a loser:

When people want to help you . . . LET them!

My beloved Tommy . . . prior to his unfortunate demise

LESSON #7

MIRACLES STILL HAPPEN!

Much as I love to help *animals*, I'll move heaven and earth to try to help the *people* I care about!

Nothing is more depressing than feeling powerless to help them when they're in a difficult spot!

33 years old is WAY too young for a diagnosis of Hodgkin's lymphoma—but it happens; and this was the path that my dear friend Kendra had to walk.

I'll never forget answering the phone and hearing her mother say: "The doctor says there's nothing they can do. You need to come now."

I couldn't believe my ears!

Kendra had just endured six months of chemotherapy like a champ, and we were all sure that she had battled and won! Only three months later, however, the cancer was BACK!

I drove six hours (from Springfield, Illinois to Kansas City, Missouri) to be with her when she got the confirmation from her oncologist that her cancer was, indeed, back—and back with a vengeance!

In a desperate, last-ditch attempt to save her life, Kendra underwent a bone marrow transplant—which, rendering her unable to fight off even the smallest infection, meant three months of forced isolation.

After the transplant, which was supposed to help, it was evident that she was instead on the decline . . . and rapidly getting worse!

I knew we were in trouble the night I received a text from her, saying: "I'm done, I'm finished fighting. I want to crawl into a hole and never come out. I can't do this anymore."

The Kendra I knew was a fighter. She would never throw in the towel unless the situation was dire indeed—which it was!

I soon learned that she was being admitted to the hospital with infection and a fever, her condition rapidly deteriorating. When the news came that she was being put on a ventilator (to allow her body an opportunity to rest), I prayed all the harder—desperately wanting to see my friend healed this side of eternity and pleaded with God to do so.

That's when the call came.

The doctor says there's nothing they can do. You need to come now.

While I raced to Kansas City as fast as my little car would go, people all over the world (from South Africa to Japan to Europe) were praying for a miracle . . .

On the way there, I spoke with Kendra's pastor, who had just seen her in the hospital—and was absolutely unwavering in his belief that she would be healed!

While at the hospital, he had asked the nurse what he should watch for. She explained the signs of the body shutting down in the dying process. "No," he explained, "I want to know the signs that she's *improving.*" His query was met with the blank stare of a nurse who insisted: "That's not going to happen, buddy!"

But he continued to pray—and *believe* . . .

He'd even gone so far as to hold a special prayer service—in which he asked all those who weren't going to pray (in faith) for her healing to LEAVE! He was that certain that help and healing were on the way!

When I arrived at the hospital, nothing could have prepared me for the heartbreaking sight of my dear friend on a vent. Her mom could see how uncomfortable I was but, full of faith, asked me to stay positive and upbeat and to talk to Kendra about all the trips that we planned to take with her in the future . . . so I did.

Incredibly enough, by the next day, to the complete and utter disbelief of all the medical professionals attending her, Kendra was suddenly (and inexplicably) beginning to show signs of *improvement!*

The doctor just shook his head as he examined her. "I have no idea why she's improving," he said. "I just can't explain it."

But I could; all our prayers were making a difference!

"Miracles DO *still* happen," I said, the doctor nodding in silent agreement as he left the room.

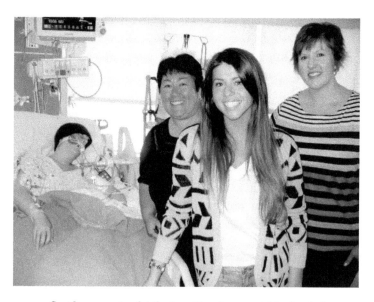

Smiling . . . in faith that Kendra would be healed

Kendra battled valiantly for 21 long hard days before she was able to go home. Today, she is cancer-free . . . and a shining testimony to all who know her!

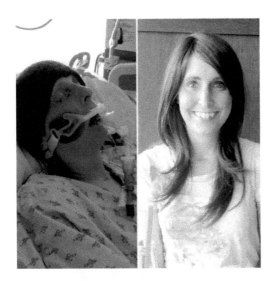

On a ventilator and . . . 21 days later!
– miracles DO still happen

Our *bodies* may fail us, but *He* never does.

When the *doctors* have no answers, *He* always does.

I am so grateful to know (and serve) a God Who's still in the business of performing miracles!

You may feel powerless to help; but, so long as you have prayer, you aren't powerless at all! There is far more power in prayer than most people will ever know.

Miracles* DO *still happen!

LESSON #8

LUXURIES ARE NOT ALWAYS LUXURIES.

Luxuries . . .

Those things that make you say, "Ahhh . . . that's *nice!*"

They don't necessarily even have to be *expensive.*

For instance, I enjoy nothing more than the luxury of sitting on the beach and listening to the waves crashing onto the shore.

Problem is—luxuries are a highly *subjective* thing. Like beauty, they really ARE in the eye of the beholder!

Most of the women I know consider a *pedicure* a real luxury and indulge themselves in one at every opportunity, particularly when they want to feel pampered.

Me? I struggle to wrap my mind around what could possibly be considered luxurious about a pedicure—which feels less like a luxury to be indulged than a torture to be endured!

You tell me what's *luxurious* about plunging your feet into a pot of boiling water!

"Feel nice, yes?" the lady says. I try to suppress the pain long enough to nod (so maybe she'll at least move along and let me suffer in silence).

I can hardly say what I'm really feeling.

Yes, ma'am—I could scarcely BE any more excited about the fact that I walked in here on my own two feet and am going to have to hobble out on the charred stumps of what's left! This is GREAT!

That's before she starts plunging that sharp metal object deep into my cuticle.

No, that doesn't hurt at all—but could you maybe stitch up that spot where all the blood is spurting out? Oh sure—by all means, use a little acetone to stop the bleeding . . . that's perfect! It really feels good.

Now she's applying a Brillo pad to the bottom of my feet (like she's scrubbing the floor of a junior high boys' locker room) while maintaining a death grip on my piggies that'll have them screaming "'Wee, wee, wee' all the way home," for sure!

Just when I think things can't possibly *get* any better, she takes what I can only assume is a cheese grater to my blistered soles!

Oh, yeahhh—having sheets of skin sheared off without benefit of anesthesia is an AMAZING experience!

But she saves the real highlight for the end—when she applies some sort of scrub potion that I am reasonably certain contains tiny shards of broken glass, rubbing it all in with rocks that have been heated to a temperature well in excess of 200 degrees*!*

Ohhh, please—could you rub just a little bit longer? I can't quite see any exposed tendons just yet . . . !

Then there was the time I inadvertently added *insult* to *injury* . . .

Having decided that I should not be the only one to experience such unparalleled pleasure, I'd gotten my *mother* into the chair.

She was enjoying the back massager when I noticed that the poor lady working on her toes was bouncing all over the place!

I grabbed the remote control and said, "Mom, I'm going to have to turn your chair down a little; you've got her bouncing all around down there while she's trying to work!"

"Oh no," the pedicurist exclaimed. "It's not your mom's fault; I have tremors!"

Well, didn't *I* feel about two feet tall! I couldn't stop apologizing—while searching frantically for an additional vat of boiling water into which to plunge my head . . . before I said something even *more* embarrassing!

Another day, I attracted a lot more attention than I wanted . . .

It had been a while since my last pedicure, so I'd somehow let myself be talked into going yet again (psyching myself into believing that my selective memory had surely blown my previous experiences all out of proportion).

Entering the shop, I took one look at the tiny little 60-pound Asian lady about to go to work on me and thought reassuringly, "How bad can this possibly be?"

Things actually got off to a pretty good start . . .

I was well into the procedure; so far, nothing was bleeding; and I even remembered to ask her to lay off the cheese grater (and was unspeakably grateful when she agreed to set it aside)!

We were coming down the home stretch when she grabbed the "Shards of Broken Glass" lotion and started rubbing it over my calves.

I was grinding my teeth and trying not to wince when, all of a sudden, her eyes widened and she began to shout, "My goodness, you regs are berry schrong!"

Being half-Asian myself, I was used to acting as my mother's interpreter—so I knew what she meant: *your legs are very strong!*

Now, in the interest of full disclosure for those of you who have never seen my *calves,* they really ARE a work of *art*—probably the one truly remarkable physical feature that I have! Thanks to a pretty intensive weight-lifting regimen when I was in college, they've been nicely-sculpted ever since—but it was nice of her to notice.

"Thank you," I said, smiling sweetly.

If only it had stopped there . . . but I was not to be so lucky!

"Hey—come here," she screamed to her colleague three chairs over. "Rook at her regs; dey no moob!" *Look at her legs; they don't move!* (Apparently most people's *jiggle*—but not *mine!)*

Those little ladies were clearly in awe—but I have never felt more like a sideshow freak in my life than I did in that moment!

So the next time a friend invites you to join them for a luxurious pedicure, don't say I didn't warn you . . .

Luxuries are not always *luxuries.*

LESSON #9

LET YOUR DEFINING MOMENTS *MAKE* YOU — NOT *BREAK* YOU.

We all have moments that can *make* or *break* us!

As a coach, I've seen countless athletes *soar*—though, just as often, I've had to watch them *flop,* which is never easy.

They may not have been my *biological* children, but I invested in them as if they were!

Even as I urged them not to let their nerves keep them from achieving their dreams, at times I could hardly keep it together myself . . . because I so wanted them to do well!

My own nerves notwithstanding, I took great pride in my ability to motivate kids to achieve more than they could ever have hoped, dreamed, or imagined!

I will never forget one particular day—when I watched an athlete experience both the agony of defeat *and* the thrill of victory . . .

Over the years, I've had the opportunity to work with a lot of outstanding athletes—but Rachel was one of the finest I have ever been privileged to coach.

In the six years that I coached Rachel, she battled a number of injuries—but she never let them break her spirit. Each time, she got back up, determined to work harder and smarter than ever!

By her senior year in high school, she had emerged as a real star of track and field, making it to the State Finals in three different events: the high jump, 400-meter dash, and the 4x400-meter relay.

Much to her disappointment and dismay, she finished in only fifth place in the high jump—but immediately began focusing on the next event.

Ranked sixth in the state as she began the last 400-meter dash of her high school career, all she needed to do to snag a medal was to finish the race—which she *did* . . . in 9th place—dead last!

The high jump competition had clearly taken a lot out of her, so she just couldn't run like she ordinarily would have. Still—a medal is a medal, right?!

Ten minutes later, I was called over the loudspeaker to report to the coaches' area.

This can't be good! I thought to myself.

It wasn't.

Rachel had been disqualified when judges determined that she had stepped on the line several times during the race—so there would be no medal after all!

It fell to me to explain all this to my top athlete. She put her head down and, as the tears rolled down her face, I stepped back to give her time and space to process it all.

Just before we began the final race of the day (our 4x400-meter relay), I knelt in front of my flickering star, saying: "Rachel, this is a defining moment in your life. Things did not go the way that you anticipated or wanted—but now you can either let this *make* you or *break* you. The choice is *yours*—but this is *your* defining moment!"

Rachel nodded in agreement and, as the race got under-way, I could see the fire in her eyes . . .

By the time the baton was passed to her, we were in third place.

She quickly passed a girl in the first turn and we were in second—where we stayed for most of the rest of the race until, in the last 100 meters, Rachel pulled up alongside the leader.

Neck-and-neck, they ran the final 100, 75, 50, 25, 10, 5 meters together—until, in the last possible moment, Rachel dove across the line to break the school record and win the State Title!

The stadium erupted in a roar as we all dissolved into a puddle of tears! To this day, that remains one of the greatest moments of my coaching career.

Rachel stepped up to the challenge, looked her defining moment in the eye—and seized it! Instead of letting her previous defeat define her, she used it to pave a path into the record books!

I still can't think about that day without remembering the words of the great Coach Vince Lombardi, noting that "the greatest accomplishment is not in never falling, but in rising again after you fall!"

When your defining moment comes, you can let it make you or break you.

The choice is yours . . .

You can't always keep from *falling* (or being *knocked*) down.

But you don't have to *stay* down! You can rise again!

Let your defining moments MAKE you,* not *BREAK you!

*Rachel in her winning moments . . . and with the
winning State Championship Squad*

LESSON #10

BE CAREFUL WHEN TRAVELING ABROAD.

As my dear friend (and co-author) Christopher never tires of pointing out, I may very well be the world's first and only "redneck Asian."

But that's what happens when Uncle Sam plants a central Illinois farm boy named Calvin Jones in Okinawa, Japan—where he falls for a girl named Keiko Keinkawa . . . their union produces a unique blend of two very distinct cultures in "yours truly."

Having grown up in the small-town of Litchfield, Illinois—I was definitely more "redneck" growing up; but, as an adult, I've had an opportunity to get in touch with my *Asian* heritage, as well.

A "Redneck Asian" with her parents

Accompanying my mother to re-visit her native home-
land has afforded me a number of experiences that have
been, um, *interesting* (to say the least)!

From my experience, Okinawans seem to be some of
the kindest and most caring people in the world. They
are also some of the bluntest!

My then-nearly-300-pound self had been in Okinawa for
only a few hours before feeling unusually self-conscious
after a succession of remarks (from relatives and strangers alike) noting my obvious fondness for food. *You very
big!* and *You eat too much yakisoba!* are but a couple that
come to mind . . .

Taking my mother shopping was an adventure in itself.
One of my biggest fears is losing her in a crowd (even
at *home*—where every other woman is NOT named

"Keiko")! In Okinawa, when I had to call out her name (one of the very few Japanese words I even know), half the crowd turned to look in response!

But it was after heading into an ice cream shop (to get *sweet potato* ice cream; you can't make this stuff up!) that things REALLY got interesting . . .

After placing our order, we were sitting there patiently awaiting what I hoped would be a frozen delight—when our number was called.

I'd no sooner jumped up to retrieve our ice cream when a woman beside me began screaming and pointing at my leg!

Assuming I must have some sort of Japanese cockroach crawling up my leg, I began to panic—when, in one quick movement, she leapt to her feet and grabbed my calf (while squealing in a volume and pitch capable of waking the dead)!

Turns out, she was just floored by the size and muscle tone of my calves (which, even at my heaviest, were always a sculpted work of art—if I do say so myself).

But *that's* what all this screaming was about?!

For the first time in my life, I understood how the bearded lady in the circus must have felt! I'd become a sideshow freak, surrounded by fascinated onlookers eager to respond to what was apparently her invitation to gather 'round and feel my calves!

I could have charged admission, but my embarrassment overrode my entrepreneurial instincts—so I fled, rushing out the door without so much as a backward glance at all my newfound fans!

Never in my life was I so happy to leave an ice cream shop (which, as a then-283-pound woman, was saying something)!

Unfortunately, my humiliation was not yet complete . . .

My uncle had gone to get the car, promising to come pick us up curbside—so you'd better bet I didn't waste a minute in yanking that car door open and thrusting my celebrity calves into the relative concealment of automotive comfort!

In my haste, however, I failed to take into account the fact that many of the cars in Okinawa look a lot alike (and, if I'm being honest—as a Westerner—so do many of the *men*).

I'd barely taken my seat when this horrible high-pitched scream emerged from the driver's seat. "No, no, no!" he said. "*Go, go, go!*

In stunned bewilderment, I tried to figure out my uncle's problem (he'd seen my calves plenty of times) . . . when it suddenly dawned on me . . . *that's **NOT** my uncle!*

I was sitting in the car of a total stranger, his eyes uncharacteristically wide with terror—as he frantically shooed me with his hand, trying to expel me so that he could be on his way . . . before "Big Momma" could come his way again!

I suspect that his life has never been the same. I also suspect that I should have just stayed in the ice cream shop—if not in central *Illinois!*

That's when I first learned that you have to **be careful when traveling abroad!** You just never know what you might be getting into (including the car of one very concerned stranger)!

LESSON #11

ALWAYS KNOW WHERE TO RUN.

For 10 years, I was privileged to teach at a school where I truly loved the staff and students alike! They were "my people" in every sense of the word and, with every passing year, I was more grateful for the opportunity to "do life" with them.

Because we were all like family, it was devastating when one of our family members (a fellow teacher) was diagnosed with an aggressive form of lung cancer in the summer of 2012.

Not only were we afraid for the life of our friend, many of us found ourselves asking God: "Why?" (One of the things I love about God is that He's okay with me asking that! My questions don't threaten Him or make Him mad!)

It's just that Mandi was so full of life . . .

She was a beautiful little *brunette* with the feistiness of a *redhead!* You did NOT want to make her mad! On the other hand, her high-pitched contagious laugh that echoed down the hallways of the school could invariably put a smile on anyone's face!

We'd all been thrilled when her future husband donned a suit of armor and literally rode into the school parking lot on a white horse to ask for her hand in marriage! She did, indeed, marry her "knight in shining armor"—a man who worked hard to make all her dreams come true!

But her real "crown jewel"—the one who could make her eyes sparkle like no other—was their son. Whenever they saw each other, they both lit up! Watching them interact was pure joy!

He was only a toddler when the devastating diagnosis came down, rocking her little family to the core!

Still, they were strong! If anyone could weather this storm together, this family could!

But Mandi was in for the fight of her life as she began an aggressive course of treatment that soon had her missing school almost as much as she was there. Truthfully, she often worked even when she shouldn't have. Her dedication to her students and her fierce determination not to let them down drove her to be there anyway. She was a real warrior—fighting not only for her own survival, but to give those kids as normal a year as she possibly could.

One morning that fall, as I watched an incident unfold on the playground, I sensed the Lord leading me to share what I'd seen with Mandi.

I tried to protest, but the Lord's leading was unmistakable.

Okay, God—I get the message . . .

So, over my lunch break, I sat down at my desk—weeping as I penned this note to my fighting friend . . .

Dear Mandi,

I know it seems weird for me to be writing you a letter when I could just pop into your room and talk, but I'm not sure I can make it through this story without losing it! Hoping to spare you a blubbering mess, I thought I'd put this in writing instead . . .

I just saw an incident on the playground that I feel the Lord wants me to share with you. I don't want you to think I'm some kind of religious nut hearing voices—but I know He wants me to share this, so here goes . . .

I was watching Sally on the swing set a moment ago. She was really pumpin' her little feet and legs, going just as high and fast as she possibly could—with all the velocity a second grader can muster, laughing and having the time of her life! (Well, you know Sally . . .)

All of a sudden, from out of nowhere, here came Carter—running at full force (not looking where he was going, as usual)—and he ran right into the path of Sally, who caught him on her downward swing, throwing him a good eight feet or so! Poor boy had no idea what had hit him as he flew through the air and landed flat on his back, the wind completely knocked out of him! I think Sally was almost as scared as he was, since neither of them saw the other coming!

It all happened SO quickly!

Before any of us could even reach Carter—he'd come to his senses and jumped up, crying and running toward the first set of open arms he saw!

When he got to the playground supervisor (who'd seen the whole thing), he just collapsed in her arms and sobbed and sobbed as she held him close!

In that moment of painful uncertainty after getting knocked down, not yet knowing if he was even going to be okay, all he knew was to run to someone who could protect him! He had to run to someone bigger than the source of his pain who could wrap their arms around him and hold him as he cried!

Mandi, you've been dealt quite a blow! You've been hit hard when you never saw it coming, and I know you're looking for a place to run! When you feel like you need to be strong but really just want to sob, RUN! Run to the arms of Jesus, and let Him hold you while you cry! Let him be your Protector and Source of comfort when no one else can!

I wish I could tell you that all this is going to be okay, but what I CAN tell you is that—even when you don't know which way is up—Jesus has got you in His arms, and He'll be with you every step of the way!

I'm still praying for your complete healing. But most of all, I'm praying that—no matter what happens—you'll always know where to run!

I love you, my friend.

Sonya

I dropped the note into Mandi's box and, a few hours later, received this sweet text:

Sonya,

Nothing has made me cry as much as reading what you wrote —but know that it was well-received and was just exactly what I needed to hear; thank you so much!

Love you!

Mandi

My sweet friend lost her battle with cancer in 2016, but she fought the good fight until then! She fought hard—and with determination! The doctors had given her only a few months to live, but she defied them all to enjoy nearly five more years.

I miss her still; but, as I remember her spirit, I say to you: may YOU always know where to run!

When you're hit hard, you need a place to run.

That's the time to run to the arms of Jesus and let Him hold you, protecting and comforting you when no one else can!

May you *always know where to run!*

Sweet Mandi with Biggest Loser *trainer Jen Widerstrom
(who visited our school in 2015)*

Bonding with Jen after a long, hard workout

Getting a "serious" picture wasn't always easy with this bunch!

Group Hike Day!

Heading to the beach with castmate Rob Guiry

I love my team so much!

Ice bath . . . OUCH!

In the Biggest Loser *dining room – you never know what might happen during a meal!*

Part of an incredible cast

*Talk about (Blue) Team Spirit – Even Damien
painted his nails blue!*

The dreaded scale

The famous Biggest Loser *gym*

The pool behind our house on the Ranch

Toma doing his best to eliminate me early in the competition

With Jen and teammate Rondalee Beardslee

With Kelly Hudson, one of the show's
amazing certified athletic trainers

LESSON #12

ALWAYS DEFEND YOUR FRIENDS.

I love country music . . . but I am not a big fan of live concerts.

I simply don't enjoy being surrounded by drunk people screaming their unrecognizable covers at the very professionals who made those songs famous in the first place!

It's just not my thing.

I did, however, decide to take a dear friend of mine to see her favorite band (Rascal Flatts) for her birthday.

We made it through the first few numbers relatively unscathed; but, unfortunately, my great relief was short-lived . . .

It wasn't long until a group of scantily-clad young girls seated directly behind us stood up (with alcoholic beverages in each hand) and launched into their incoherent cover versions.

Recognizing that they had paid for their tickets just like we had, I tried to remain calm—but, inwardly, I was increasingly agitated by their horrific howling!

Still, I managed to keep my cool until one of them decided to invade my space . . .

Trying to get comfortable, I had just started to put my arm on the back of my friend's seat when I discovered the space was already occupied . . . by the FEET of the charming little lady directly behind us!

I turned to confront the girl—who was texting so frantically I feared her thumbs might fall off!

"Excuse me," I said, "I just wanted to put my arm here on the back of the seat."

Never moving her feet, she continued to text—looking up from her phone just long enough to roll her eyes!

Tell me she did NOT just roll her eyes at me! Girrrlll . . . somebody better hold me back!

Exercising all the self-restraint I could muster, I simply grabbed her feet and returned them to the floor where they belonged!

Calm was momentarily restored (crisis averted) . . . until she again jumped up, screaming some semblance of the song and dancing with such wild abandon that her crossbody purse was thumping my friend in the back of the head!

Now, you need to know that I really *love* my friends and would do anything in my power to protect them! (You see where this is going, right?)

I tried to tell myself that this may have been an accident, but she continued to dance—thrusting my dear friend's head forward with growing force!

At this point, after asking her politely to stop (TWICE), I'd had enough! This was no accident! It was *ON* now!

In one swift pull, I grabbed both of her purse straps and pulled her head down; her behind flying up in the air as she bucked in an attempt to break free!

The harder she bucked, the more tightly I reined her in!

As she continued bucking like a bronco, I addressed the little filly in my most authoritative manner, my tone making it clear that I would tolerate no further nonsense.

"Look, little girl," I said, "I don't know what your problem is—but, if you hit my friend in the back of the head with your purse one more time, I'm going to pick you up and throw you four rows forward . . . do I make myself clear?"

Continuing to buck, she could manage no more than a grunt—as she persisted in trying to free herself from my grasp.

Repeating my threat, I tightened my grip . . . until she finally relented and agreed to my terms.

I had no sooner let go of the reins than she proceeded to beat the hastiest retreat I've ever seen in my life (with expletives flying every step of the way)!

I wish I could tell you that a chastened (and sober) young lady returned in humility and contrition a few minutes later to request (and receive) my forgiveness . . . before I led her in the "Sinner's Prayer" to receive Christ!

Unfortunately, I never saw her again—though I have thought about that encounter many times since.

I really wasn't trying to be a bully, but there are times when bullies have to BE bullied in defense of those you love!

Always defend your friends! If you're not willing to do *that*, then they need to find a better friend!

LESSON #13

GET UNCOMFORTABLE WITH BEING COMFORTABLE.

One of the things hammered into me by my trainer during my time on *The Biggest Loser* was the need to "*get* uncomfortable and *stay* uncomfortable!"

I had no idea how long (or how hard) I'd been working to keep myself comfortable (and disguise any discomfort) until I started thinking back . . .

In 2013, my coaching team and I were privileged to lead our junior high softball team to the state championship—which we just knew we could WIN!

This was a team that would make any coach's mouth water; they were just that good!

Heading into the championship, they were under a tremendous amount of pressure—but they handled it all with grace and did indeed WIN the whole thing, emerging as the Illinois State Champions!

I couldn't have been prouder—until, looking at the coverage in the newspaper, I spotted a picture that haunted me so badly that it eventually drove me to change my life!

This one picture forced me to realize that *something* HAD to change!

It may not be obvious to *you*, so let me tell you what *I* see when I look at this photo . . .

The scenario was this: we'd been down three runs in the bottom of the fifth inning with a score of 5-2. I had two runners (on first and second) and my center fielder was up to bat with one out.

If we didn't win this game, it was all over—so we had a lot riding on these next few minutes.

My center fielder hit a solid line drive that enabled my two runners to make it home, raising the score to a more competitive 5-4.

The picture was snapped in one of the biggest coaching moments of my life—as I was frantically waving my batter in to win the game!

Most people who looked at this saw only a great picture.

What I saw made me cringe.

You'll notice that my right hand is waving my runner around the bases—but look closely at my left . . .

Do you see it?

In this, the biggest coaching moment of my life (to that point), I was subconsciously tugging on my shirt to keep it from exposing my fat—all in a desperate attempt to avoid being made to feel *uncomfortable!*

The minute I saw this picture, I knew that I had allowed negative self-talk to rule my life for far too long and that *something* HAD to change!

This one picture made me SO uncomfortable that I was willing to endure whatever *additional* discomfort might prove necessary (even the eventual discomfort of exposing my source of deepest shame on national television) in order to make a lasting change in my life!

The need for comfort can be one of your greatest enemies.

It can keep you from becoming your BEST—and hold you back from a wonderful life (of which you've hardly dared dream)!

But allowing yourself to be made *uncomfortable* is the first step toward getting better!

Staying comfortable will cripple you—but getting *uncomfortable* can be the necessary agent of change to lead you to the life you've always longed for!

So, in the immortal words of my trainer: ***get uncomfortable with being comfortable!***

Trust me—it's one of the greatest gifts you can ever give yourself.

The thrill of victory! 2013 State Champs

LESSON #14

SOMETIMES YOU'VE GOT TO TAKE A CHANCE.

Like any aspiring leader, I was spending my free time one afternoon scrolling through Facebook . . . when I stumbled across a post from NBC's hit reality TV show, *The Biggest Loser*—then about to begin casting for its 16th season!

I had loved this show and watched it religiously since its inception—usually with a big ol' pizza in my lap and a two-liter of soda in my hand—just imagining how tough it would be to compete! (Boy, was I ever right about *that!)*

In fact, speaking of Facebook—way back in 2009, I'd actually penned a Facebook post listing "25 Random Things No One Knows About Me" . . . with #10 on the list being my secret desire to compete on *The Biggest Loser.*

25 Random Things

January 29, 2009 at 9:55pm

Rules: Once you've been tagged, you are supposed to write a note with 25 random things, facts, habits, or goals about you. At the end, choose 25 people to be tagged. You have to tag the person who tagged you. If I tagged you, it's because I want to know more about you.

> 10) I secretly desire to be a contestant on the Biggest Loser. (I guess it's not a secret anymore). Somethin' about watchin' overweight folks in spandex and sports bras that really jazzes me, I guess. Eeewww...

As only the Lord could have ordained it, I posted that at 9:55 p.m. on January 29, 2009—exactly six years (right down to the day, hour, and *minute*) before my photo-finish loss on the season finale of The Biggest Loser's 16th season! (Don't tell ME that is a coincidence! As one of my pastor friends likes to say: "There's no such thing as *coincidence* . . . only *evidence* of GOD'S *Providence!"*)

Anyway—that original post from *The Biggest Loser* casting team said that they were looking for former *athletes* . . .

Being a two-time collegiate All-American in fast-pitch softball from Greenville University (and having played both semi-professional softball and collegiate varsity soccer), I figured I fit the bill.

Besides—what did I have to *lose?!*

"Why not take a chance?" I thought. "Just fill out the application!"

So I did—and the *rest*, as they say, is *history!*

Little did I know that one decision would change the course of my life!

So, next time you feel a similar nudge, go ahead . . . *take a chance!*

You just never know what God may have in store for *YOU!*

LESSON #15

DON'T LET FEAR DETERMINE YOUR FUTURE!

Who DOES this?!

Those words kept running through my head as I approached the casting finals for *The Biggest Loser.*

Who dons Spandex and a sports bra (at 283 pounds, no less) and struts around a stage on national television for all of America to see—all in the name of losing weight?!

I almost talked myself out of going.

You have a great life already, that little voice in my head kept saying. *A great career, great family, great friends . . . why would you want to risk all that and subject yourself to potential ridicule and humiliation?!*

Besides, I felt like losing weight was something that I should be able to do on my own! Granted, over 30+ years, I had tried pretty much everything (without success), but still . . .

All the way to the airport, I was still trying to talk myself out of boarding that plane to L.A.! *This is CRAZY . . . isn't it?*

What's crazy is that I nearly missed the opportunity to learn that we must never let our destiny be dictated by fear!

Because that's really what it all boiled down to: ***FEAR!***

I was afraid!

- Afraid to leave my comfortable life behind for an indeterminate time

- Afraid of what would happen if I made it onto the show (and even more afraid of what would happen if I *didn't*)

- Afraid of being open and transparent for all the world to see—and of having to face the emotion all of that would bring

- Afraid of letting everyone down . . .

I was so desperately afraid . . . that my fear began to overtake me— and I *almost* didn't get on the plane that morning.

But when you look at these "before-and-after" pictures, I think you'll understand why I'm so glad I did . . .

The pictures on the left were taken after I boarded the plane that morning—getting ready to head to L.A. on the biggest, scariest adventure of my life. The pictures on the right were taken a few months later—on the other side of that adventure.

In many ways, that is not the same woman in those two sets of pictures.

The woman on the left may be smiling but is using that smile to mask the fact that she is deeply embarrassed by what she has become and absolutely hates who she is. Still, I can't help but honor that woman—whose courageous decision to board the plane *that* day helped make me who I am now, on *this* day.

Because, *today,* I am that woman on the right. A woman who is proud of having faced her fears and accepted the challenge to change. A woman who now feels good about who she is as a person—filled with newfound confidence and using her journey to health and wellness to impact as many *others* as possible.

When I look at these pictures, I shudder to think of all that I could have missed, had I been foolish enough to let fear determine my future!

What great adventure are YOU talking yourself out of because of *your* fear?

Face your fear. Go ahead and take that first step. (Trust me—that back foot will follow.)

Fear will cripple you if you let it. On the other hand, it can provide you with a pretty incredible adrenaline rush!

Fear can be a debilitating foe . . . or your dearest friend—your choice!

The Bible says (in Romans 8:37) that the power of Christ compels us to be "more than conquerors"—which means that He will enable YOU to conquer *your* fear!

Don't let the enemy use your fear to rob you of the great adventures the Father has planned for you!

Don't let fear determine your future!

LESSON #16

BEING ALONE ISN'T *ALWAYS* A BAD THING.

One thing I hadn't anticipated when trying out for a spot on *The Biggest Loser* was that, during casting finals, I would have to spend nearly two weeks completely sequestered in a hotel room!

And when I say "sequestration"—well, *solitary confinement* would be more like it!

I was not allowed to leave my room without permission (nor did I even have a key). I was to have no contact with other potential contestants—not even a look in their direction, much less any actual conversation.

For a sanguine extrovert like me, sequestration sounded like anything BUT fun! After all, my self-diagnosed ADHD (with an emphasis on the "H") means that I *live* for interaction with others!

Unbeknownst to me, however, this time alone would prove to be one of the most valuable experiences of my life—and essential preparation for the adventure on which I was about to embark.

You see, my real challenge on *The Biggest Loser* would not be one of weight loss. (You can't be a contestant on that show and NOT lose weight!) The real battle would be fought on a mental, spiritual, and emotional plane—and would require a level of toughness that I had never known.

By the grace of God, those days of sequestration in a hotel room provided me with the time and space necessary to prepare myself for the journey that lay ahead.

Once I was no longer able to communicate with *others,* I was forced to focus all my energy toward communicating with *God.*

Soon, I began to use that time to settle my spirit and seek out God's direction for the path that was about to unfold.

I spent nearly every single one of those days reading and memorizing Scripture and engaging in rich and meaningful time of personal worship and prayer. It was, quite honestly, the single best thing I've ever done for myself! In fact, I don't ever again want to spend so much time with others that I forget about spending time with God.

Although it was difficult for me to be out of communication with others, it ultimately proved to be a blessing because it allowed me to disconnect from everything around me and focus on the only One Who truly matters!

Being alone isn't always a bad thing . . . particularly if that's what it takes to help you realize that, as a *believer*, you are never truly alone—because of the powerful presence of the One Who is within you!

LESSON #17

LISTEN TO THE STILL, SMALL VOICE.

Day Two on *The Biggest Loser* Ranch was a day I will never forget: the day of the dreaded Sand Dune Challenge!

Sand Mountain.

Just typing those words sends chills running up and down my spine.

It was a challenge like none I've ever faced and ended with a result I would never have anticipated.

As a *Biggest Loser* fan from the beginning, I've seen a lot of trainers come and go—but, by the time I got to the show, three were long-standing: Bob Harper, Jillian Michaels, and Dolvett Quince. After watching them for several seasons, I felt like I knew each of them—their training styles and techniques—and there was no doubt in my mind who I would choose to be MY trainer if I managed to score a spot on the show: Dolvett was my man!

I didn't know the man, of course—but felt I knew all I needed to know: he was gorgeous, single, and wearing a smile designed to make any heart race! Factor in the genuine care and concern he seemed to show for his teams (not to mention abdominal muscles that I firmly believe the Lord Himself chiseled out on the eighth day of Creation) and there could be no other choice for me! I had to have Dolvett! *"Grant it, Jesus"* was my plea!

But there were some major surprises in store.

After being cast on the show, we all headed out to begin filming at the L.A. Coliseum, where we would meet our trainers for the first time. When we got there, however, there was no sign of Bob Harper OR Jillian Michaels! Both had been replaced . . . by two brand-new trainers I'd never even *heard* of: Jessie Pavelka and Jen Widerstrom. Who are they? Who knew if either of them was even any good?

To my enormous relief, however, Dolvett remained—standing right there in front of me, live and in-the-GLORIOUS-flesh! Hallelujah, thank You Jesus—my man was still on the show!

We caught our first glimpse of the three trainers as they ran down the stairs into the Coliseum and over to us, giving each of us a "high five" as they took their spots right in front of us.

Ladies—if I may speak to the female population for just a moment—it gives me great pleasure to inform you that Dolvett is even better-looking up close than he is from a distance! And boy, does he *smell* GOOOOOODD! One big whiff of his cologne when he came whizzing past me and I was smitten! "Yummy!" I said. "THAT'S *my* trainer!"

Host Alison Sweeney formally introduced the trio of trainers—as each took a few minutes to talk to us about their particular passions and individual training styles.

In that moment, I was fairly certain that *my* passion was Dolvett; HE was *my* style! I could feel my heart rate increasing the minute he opened his mouth and started to speak!

Then Jessie began talking and I thought, "Man, *he's* hot too! I could totally be on *his* team!"

Finally, it was Jen's turn.

She talked about her incessant drive to help people improve and explained that, for her, this was a very personal mission. Because she wanted to build—not just a team—but a family, she promised that she would be right by our side every step of the way.

And in that moment, I sensed the Lord speaking to my heart: "SHE will be your trainer!"

I, however, was prepared to argue.

"Excuse me?" I said. "Lord, You have seen Dolvett's abdominal muscles, right?! Hello?! Shouldn't *he* be my trainer?"

I'm not sure, but I think the Lord might have rolled His eyes as He again spoke to my heart—even *more* clearly this time: "Jen will be your trainer."

Two days later, I was standing at the foot of Sand Mountain—facing the biggest challenge of my life! As a former collegiate and semi-professional athlete, I'm no stranger to tough workouts. I have endured workout sessions that would have left most people in the dust. But nothing—and I do mean nothing—has ever challenged me physically like Sand Mountain!

I'd seen this massive mountain of sand in previous seasons, but contestants didn't ordinarily face this challenge until later in the season—once they'd gotten into shape. Being former athletes, however, we were expected to tackle it on our first challenge!

The challenge was to scale this sandy mountain (with a gigantic medicine ball in hand) while simultaneously working through a daunting obstacle course in the sand! We had to make it all the way to the top to claim one of the 18 spots on the show—and there were *20* of us at the starting gate! The first 18 to stake out the summit would secure a spot and get to choose their trainer; the tardy twosome lagging behind would get to start *packing* . . . for the trip home!

As we prepared to start that steep scale in the sand, Ali posed a provocative question: If we made it all the way up to earn the privilege of choosing our trainers, whom would we choose?

"Ali," I said, "if you'd asked me that question a week ago, without any hesitation, I'd have said 'Dolvett'. But, the other night at the Coliseum, I felt an instant connection with Jen that I can't even explain . . . so if I make it up this mountain today, I'll choose Jen."

A few others gave their answers as well; then Ali said "GO," and we were off!

The burning sand was so incredibly fine that it felt like my feet were being swallowed with each step. I struggled to make it up the first hill over three sets of large yellow obstacles.

Successfully surmounting all three obstacles, I'd finished only the first side of the mountain and now had to wind through a maze back downhill. Only when I arrived all the way back at the bottom could I begin the grueling trek up the last and longest part of the mountain. There, after climbing under a long volleyball net, I faced an additional three sets of obstacles and had to weave my way through a set of poles before finally throwing my ball into the court of the trainer of my choice!

Realizing that I was somewhere in the middle of the pack as I started up that last hill, I struggled painfully to get over those final obstacles. Tossing the ball over the first one, I pulled myself over; then staggered on to the next, somehow managing to pull myself over once again—but I was fading fast. I eventually made it over that third and final obstacle, but had absolutely no strength left! I mean none. I was utterly wiped out.

Physically, I didn't think that I could take another step if my life depended on it!

Struggling not to pass out, I stretched out over that big medicine ball, trying to summon any ounce of strength I could—but there was simply no more to be had.

In frantic desperation, I began to pray. "Lord," I pleaded, "I didn't come this far to go home now. Please, Father— please give me the strength to make it the rest of the way up this mountain! I know that I can do ALL things through You because You give me the strength!" I was begging now. "Father, *please* help me make it up this mountain to make it on Jen's team."

At that moment, I heard my name.

"Sonya!" the voice screamed. "Sonya!"

I looked up to see where it was coming from.

"*Sonya!*"

It was Jen.

My eyes locked with hers, as she yelled: "You said you wanted me as your trainer, now come get me! LET'S GO!"

Picking up the ball, I felt a sudden surge of strength beginning to return as I put one foot in front of the other, trudging up the last half of that mountain. Step by step, I climbed and zigzagged through those final poles in the sand, made it to the top, and tossed my ball into the White Team's court . . . where Jen awaited.

Never so glad to see someone in my life, I literally collapsed into her arms when I got to the top. Then she took my face in her hands and did something I'll never forget.

"Honey," she said, "you DID it! I *knew* you could! And that connection you talked about a minute ago? I felt it too . . . and this starts our journey *together!*"

And so it did.

Jen Widerstrom – best trainer on the planet . . . and a friend who changed the course of my life

Thus began a wonderful journey to not just *fitness*, but *friendship!* Without question, choosing Jen Widerstrom as my trainer was the best decision that I made while on *The Biggest Loser*. Actually, *I* didn't make it. Truth is, she was chosen *for* me—by One Who knew better than I!

Things don't always go the way we plan.

We sometimes have to sacrifice what looks really good in the moment (Dolvett's abs) for what's going to be BEST (choosing Jen as my trainer) in the long run.

But we first have to **listen for the still, small voice** of the only One Who knows best!

HE will never disappoint. In fact, His Word tells us that He will do "exceedingly, abundantly more than we could ever hope or imagine."

In my personal journey, I've found that to be true over and over again.

Listen . . . and *follow*. I promise you won't be disappointed.

LESSON #18

WORK LIKE IT DEPENDS ON *YOU;*
PRAY LIKE IT DEPENDS ON *GOD!*

During my time as a contestant on *The Biggest Loser,* there were two books which I read every single day—without fail.

First and foremost, obviously, was my Bible—but the other was a book called *Draw the Circle.*

Written by Dr. Mark Batterson, a pastor in the D.C. area, *Draw the Circle* is essentially a challenge to 40 consecutive days of focused prayer.

My first encounter with the book was when I was "praying circles" around my friend Kendra during her battle with Hodgkin's lymphoma (described in Chapter Seven). After experiencing the power of prayer so dramatically during that whole episode, I felt like *Draw the Circle* would be a valuable tool in my arsenal as I went into one of the biggest battles of my life on *The Biggest Loser.* So, I planted it in my suitcase, right beneath my Bible!

At the time, I still had no idea just how dramatically it was going to transform my life. At this point, however, I'd have to say that, with the exception of the Bible itself, no book has ever impacted my life so greatly!

Early in my *Biggest Loser* journey (while still sequestered in the hotel during casting finals, actually), I was sitting in my room one day reading Batterson's book. All of a sudden, the following words stopped me in my tracks: "We need to work like it depends on us, but we also need to pray like it depends on God."[1]

Work like it depends on you and pray like it depends on God.

Those 13 words would become my "mantra" (and life-line) for my entire time on the show, as I determined to *work* like it depended on me (during what would be the most difficult workouts of my life) . . . and to *pray* like it depended on GOD—which it did! (I wound up praying pretty much every waking moment of my life—but especially on weigh-in days . . . when we never knew which of us might be going home!)

But, from the very beginning, I resolved to work hard—and pray even harder—as I officially became a contestant and moved onto *The Biggest Loser* Ranch.

Technically part of the King Gillette Ranch (which once belonged to the razor blade magnate), the show's set is a beautiful 588-acres just outside Malibu, California.

Surrounded by the Santa Monica Mountains and only a stone's throw from the Pacific Ocean, this impressive property would be my home for four of the hardest (but happiest) months of my life!

The Ranch is surrounded by a paved path that encircles the entire campus. Every morning, I would "circle" the property in prayer. This "prayer walk" was not part of my fitness routine, mind you—but simply a time for me to prepare my spirit for the day.

The path on which I circled the ranch each morning on my "prayer walk"

Walking leisurely, I would just talk to God as if He were walking right beside me—about my friends back home, my family, my church and school district, and people I cared about who did not yet know Christ. Oh yeah—I prayed for my journey on *The Biggest Loser* too, of course!

Every day, I asked God to specifically "order my steps"—making sure that I would honor Him in both word and deed. I asked Him to calm my nerves, steady my heart, and give me strength to make it through the workouts. I basically just talked to Him about any and every thing that came to mind and asked Him to prepare me for whatever might be ahead.

Before long, I realized that this "circling the Ranch" in prayer had become the most important part of my day!

That's not to take anything away from the workouts. Trust me, I put in the time and did the work there too!

Every day, I worked like it all depended on me—giving it my all in the gym and working out like I had never worked out before (*The Biggest Loser* made my workouts as a college athlete seem like a walk in the park, by comparison)!

But hard as I worked, I prayed even harder. I prayed like it all depended on God (which it did)!

That kept my priorities and perspective in line and was ultimately my recipe for success!

But recipes are made for sharing, so I offer you this one (one of my favorites) from Mark Batterson: ***Work like it depends on you, but pray like it depends on God!***

LESSON #19

A CORD OF THREE STRANDS IS NOT EASILY BROKEN.

As any of you who watched Season 16 of *The Biggest Loser* know, I was blessed to be part of an unusually close-knit team!

Those of us on the White Team began as friends, but quickly became family. We are still in touch, and will forever be part of each others' lives.

I don't think any of us could have envisioned the strong relationships that developed, and I give our trainer, Jen Widerstrom, a lot of the credit. She helped us see each other more as friends/family than competitors.

Early on in our journey, Jen led us on a team hike up to Inspiration Point—one of those beautiful places on the Ranch where you can hardly help but feel closer to God . . . once you finally get there!

We'd no sooner made it to Inspiration Point than I felt compelled to share a passage of Scripture with the team that I felt sure would be an inspiration to all of us.

Solomon writes in Ecclesiastes 4 (NLT): "Two people are better off than one, for they can help each other succeed. If one person falls, the other can reach out and help. But someone who falls alone is in real trouble . . . a person standing alone can be attacked and defeated, but two can stand back-to-back and conquer. Three are even better, for a cord of three strands is not easily broken!"

A cord of three strands is not easily broken. That certainly struck a chord with me (pun intended)!

As I shared that Scripture with the team, we all agreed that adopting this philosophy could only make us stronger.

The first strand of our three-stranded cord was that of seven truly stellar individuals – each bringing something unique to the group . . .

Toma was a solid man of integrity and honor who brought a quiet confidence paired with a work ethic that was unmatched. His kindness was inspiring and served to calm many a storm (though his kindness should never be mistaken for weakness . . . as he effectively demonstrated when he kicked my butt on national television)!

JJ had an amazingly loving spirit and brought a laughter that was contagious. His fierce fervor and zeal for life motivated us all as he compelled us to lay it on the line every single day and push beyond our limits to attain things we would never have believed possible!

Rondalee had an unmatched intensity and desire to win which fueled a fierce competitiveness that stirred each of us to reach for our potential. But it was her gentle encouragement that helped each of us believe . . . both in each *other* and in *ourselves.*

Matt brought a genuine love and affection that quietly lifted us up in ways he was not always even aware. He believed in us even when we didn't, and freely gave of himself to help us get back on track.

Woody was our "all-in" teammate who had a remarkable knack for tugging at our heartstrings in a way that enabled *us* to face challenges as courageously as *he* did! He made us proud to be part of his family and consistently drove us with his passion.

Jen played the most critical role of all as our coach! She created an incredible level of trust that enabled us to face inner demons we didn't even know were there! She persistently pushed us to press past the pain to pursue the prospect of a healthier and happier version of ourselves. Equal parts educator and encourager, she served as both our backbone and buddy!

The second strand was the team itself, and the unparalleled strength that we had *together.*

Without question, however, our third and strongest strand was God, Who brought each of us together and served as our ultimate Source of strength (both individually and collectively)!

From my perspective, the White Team enjoyed unprecedented strength and success precisely because of our friendship and camaraderie.

We recognized that each individual played a significant part.

We discovered that the team really WAS stronger than the individual.

We recognized that the God Who put us all together was the real Source of our bond.

We were unquestionably better and stronger together because as the ancient words of Scripture so rightly observe: *a cord of three strands is not easily broken!*

More than a team, we became a family

LESSON #20

CHAMPIONS AREN'T *CREATED* IN THE *RING;* THAT'S SIMPLY WHERE THEY'RE *CROWNED!*

I have such enormous respect for champions!

Many of my greatest personal heroes are those who stand out as undisputed champions in their field.

I'm thinking of people like:

Michael Jordan—a two-time Olympic gold medalist in basketball who, after 15 glorious seasons in the NBA, is generally regarded as the greatest basketball player of all time!

Pat Summitt—the American women's college basketball head coach who, before her early retirement (to battle Alzheimer's), accrued 1,098 career wins, the most in college basketball history!

John Wooden—the "Wizard of Westwood" who, in his twelve years as head basketball coach at UCLA, saw the Bruins to 10 NCAA national championships (including a record seven-in-a-row) and was the first person ever to be inducted into the Basketball Hall of Fame as both a *player* and a *coach!*

Muhammad Ali—universally regarded as one of the greatest athletes of the 20th century, the heavyweight boxing champion of the world had a career record of 56 wins, 5 losses and 37 knockouts. Even after Parkinson's disease reduced "the Greatest" to a mere shadow of his former self, he was still known as "the Champ" . . . for good reason!

And I have unbounded admiration for the entire **U.S. Olympic Softball Team** of 1996, 2000 and 2004 (one of whose members, *Lori Harrigan-Mack*, would become a dear personal friend during our time as fellow contestants on *The Biggest Loser*).

With members of the Gold Medal U.S. Olympic Softball Team. Privileged to stand among champions

But, when any of these heroes come to mind, I'm forced to acknowledge that their championships weren't really won in the ring or on the court or field—but in all the preparation leading up to it!

They became champions in the loneliness of the gym at 5 A.M. practice sessions or shooting baskets long after midnight—in a never-ending quest to perfect their game!

You and I typically see only the glory at the end—but forget about all the guts it takes (behind the scenes) to get to that point, when no one is watching.

In fact, it's the things we do when no one else is watching that ultimately matter most! That's where real champions are forged!

One way or another, everything you do today makes a difference in your tomorrow!

When someone asks you to do something; and you decide to cut corners or only do a halfway job (thinking that no one else will ever know the difference), that matters.

Even if no one *else* knows, YOU will—and, in time, you'll discover that's really what matters most!

I think about all the times over the course of my life that I cut corners, then struggled to sleep at night—knowing I'd not done the right thing.

I attribute much of my success on *The Biggest Loser* to my unwavering commitment to the endlessly monotonous cardio prescribed by my trainer. I can't tell you how often, when she put me on the elliptical machine for an hour, I wanted so badly to step off a few minutes short.

She would never have known—nor would the *rest* of my team, but I would have. There was no way I could live with that! Not when they were all counting on me to keep us in competition as long as possible. That drove me to complete every minute of every workout (and go even *beyond* what was expected).

I was determined to get to the Finale knowing that I'd done everything in my power to win. Anything less and I could never have forgiven myself!

You have what it takes to be a champion too—but you'll have to put in the time (and effort) that it takes to make your dreams a reality!

When you've done everything you possibly can—then, one way or another, you'll be a champion. And no one can ever take that away from you!

Just remember: the *prize* is ultimately won in the *practice!*

Champions aren't *created* in the ring; that's simply where they're *crowned!*

LESSON #21

OTHER PEOPLE LOVE YOU; *YOU* SHOULD LOVE YOU TOO!

It was my very first night on *The Biggest Loser*.

I was standing on the scale in the L.A. Coliseum at 283 pounds when it dawned on me that I had absolutely no clue how I'd gotten to be so grossly overweight.

I mean—I had a great life: a wonderful career, a beautiful home, and a tremendous support system made up of the most amazing family and friends.

So why couldn't I get my weight under control?!

It took me a full eight weeks to figure that out.

The epiphany finally came, courtesy of my insightful trainer . . .

Jen and I were walking around the Ranch, talking about my journey on the show. I confessed to her that I really still didn't understand how I had let my weight get so out of control.

That's when she suddenly stopped me in my tracks and said, "Sonya, you really don't know how you got to be 283 pounds? Well, let me tell you: *everyone loves you . . . but YOU!* If you can ever learn to love you like everyone *else* loves you, then you'll be absolutely unstoppable!"

That's when the light bulb went on and, all of a sudden, I got it! I *finally* got it!

She was right.

I *didn't* love me.

Not even a little.

As a matter of fact . . . I didn't even *like* me.

I'd made it my business to make everyone *else* happy . . . rather than have to focus on or try to figure out why *I* was so unhappy!

I suddenly remembered that, on my 39th birthday, my dear friend Jeni had urged me to give a gift to myself by going just 24 hours without saying a single negative thing about myself. I refused even to consider it.

I hated who I was.

But Jen was right: virtually everyone I knew *did* love me.

In fact, when I got back home, some of the most difficult conversations were with multiple people who said,
"Sonya, I never knew . . . I never knew you felt so badly
about who you were! *I* loved you and just assumed *you*
did too! How could you *not?!* You're one of the most
incredible people I know!"

On the walk with Jen that day, I resolved that from that
point forward I would extend the same grace and mercy
to *myself* that I did not hesitate to extend to *others.*

- *I would never tell a friend that she was **fat.***

- *I would never tell a friend she was **ugly.***

- *I would never tell a friend she **didn't matter.***

I would never say those things to ANYONE – friend
or foe!

So why was it okay for me to say that to (or even believe
that about) *myself?*

IT *WASN'T!* That was a real turning point in my healing—as I began, for the first time, to believe God when
He says in His Word that *I am fearfully and wonderfully made.*

God doesn't make junk.

You and I are made in the image of God—and He made
us exactly the way He wanted us!

I want YOU to believe that for *yourself!*

God's Word is clear: you have been bought for a price (the incredibly high price of Christ's own life)! According to Romans 8:37, He has made us "more than conquerors," and He says you are better than you think . . . just because He *says* so! You are worth what He says, and He has assigned you ultimate, infinite worth and value!

It's a vicious lie from the enemy (who hates you and wants to tear you down and destroy you) that you don't matter! Don't you believe it . . . because *God* says otherwise!

One of the greatest moments of my life came when it finally dawned on me that all these other people loved me for a reason . . . and maybe I should too!

Jesus loved YOU enough to die for you . . . so don't tell me you're not loved—or worth loving!

He LOVES you; you should love you too!

A beautiful day with Jen and Woody

A memorable night with Toma and Jen

Couldn't pass up the chance to wear Lori's three gold medals

Playing a little sand volleyball with the gang

Dinner with Jen and Lori Harrigan-Mack

Enjoying life with cast and crew alike

I think Heaven may look a lot like this!

Lori and I spending some downtime on an "off" night with cast wranglers Kristen Mearns and Kasey Bates

Our fearless leaders in Kauai

Photobombed by Rob during my shower with Dolvett!

The gang in Kauai

We don't want to leave Hawaii

With Dolvett in Kauai

With Jen . . . after one of our most meaningful sessions

With Kelly and Lori - ALOHA!

With the beautiful Ali in Kauai

With two of my guys – Toma and Woody

So many unforgettable memories

LESSON #22

ATTITUDE IS EVERYTHING.

At heart, I am—and always will be—a coach!

In my 20 years of coaching, I invariably created a play-book for each of my athletes which, without exception, always included this little Charles Swindoll poem on attitude . . . that utterly transformed mine.

*The longer I live, the more I realize the importance
of choosing the right attitude in life.*

*Attitude is more important than facts.
It is more important than your past;
more important than your education or
financial situation;
more important than your circumstances, your successes,
or your failures;
more important than what other people think, say, or do;*

It is more important than your appearance,
your giftedness, or your skills.

It will make or break a company.
It will cause a church to soar or sink.
It will make the difference between a happy home
or a miserable home.

You have a choice each day regarding the attitude you
will embrace.
Life is like a violin.

You can focus on the broken strings that dangle,
or you can play your life's melody on the one that remains.
You cannot change the years that have passed,
nor can you change the daily tick of the clock.
You cannot change the pace of your march toward
your death.
You cannot change the decisions or the reactions
of other people.
And you certainly cannot change the inevitable.
Those are the strings that dangle!
What you CAN do is play on the one string that remains
– your attitude.

I am convinced that life is 10% what happens to me
and 90% how I react to it.
The same is true for you.[2]

Wow . . . Swindoll really hit the nail on the head!

Life is 10% what happens to you . . . and 90% how you
react to it.

Whatever you're going through—whether at home or work—you really have only one decision to make.

Are you going to have a good or bad attitude about it?

The choice is yours.

You can't control your circumstances—or the way others treat you.

With the exception of certain limitations, you really can't control the phone calls or e-mails you receive.

Most things in life, to be honest, are completely beyond your control.

But you have complete and total control over your attitude.

The late Zig Ziglar had it right when he said that: "Your *attitude*, not your *aptitude*, will determine your *altitude*."

Your attitude will make you or break you.

Your attitude will drive your destiny.

Attitude really ***IS everything!***

LESSON #23

THERE'S NOTHING SPANX & DUCT TAPE CAN'T FIX.

The things a girl will do to look SKINNY! I mean, I've never met a *guy* who'd strap himself into a corset just to hide his oversized belly, but my hat's off to the first one willing to try. *Women* have been doing this sort of thing for centuries!

Of course, at 283 pounds, compression garments were the last thing on my mind! The piece capable of making me look like I'd suddenly dropped 100 pounds had not yet been invented, so why would I want to subject myself to that kind of torture? What was the point?

At that point in my life, my vanity had taken a backseat for so long I wasn't even thinking along those lines—occasionally to the dismay of those who loved me!

While in casting finals, for instance, I kept getting texts from my best friend Jeni—begging me to spend a little of my free time by the pool tanning my titanic tummy! "When's the last time that stomach's seen any sunlight?" she teased. "Think of your friends before blinding us all on national TV with the whiteness of that belly!"

Everyone needs a friend who loves you enough to tell you the truth! Proverbs 27:17 (NLT) says, "As iron sharpens iron, so a friend sharpens a friend." My friend had a point—and it was sharp!

Unfortunately, *I* wasn't sharp enough to *take* her advice!

Months later, when I returned home from the show, I discovered to my horror that even my oldest and dearest friends were referring to my wardrobe at my original weigh-in as my "Oreo outfit."

You know—black on top, black on bottom with a lot of really white stuff in the middle? Yeah, that was me! Just call me "Double Stuf"!

Fortunately, when we first started filming *The Biggest Loser,* the production team didn't want us in any kind of compression gear. At that point, I think the goal was to just sort of "let it all hang out," shall we say. And, with 283 pounds on my 5'4" frame, there was a LOT to hang out!

It wasn't until much later in the season that there was any mention of minimizers. But, eventually, there came such a day—soon after we entered the "singles" phase of the competition . . .

The day *began* like that of any *other* weigh-in day. There was absolutely no warning how abruptly life was about to change when Alicia, from our wonderful wardrobe team, walked into the kitchen that morning.

I typically looked forward to her arrival, as she had always done everything in her power to help me feel good about myself. But, boy, was THAT about to change!

Without a word, she handed me a hanger holding what looked like a pair of high wasted shorts for a toddler! I took one look at this mystery wear and asked in wide-eyed wonderment: "Who's gonna wear THAT?!"

"YOU ARE!" she said. "This is for you to wear under your weigh-in tank top."

"Aren't you cute?" I said. "How in the world am I supposed to get all of *THIS* (motioning to my massive mid-section) . . . into *THAT?!*"

"Trust me," she said with a laugh. "It'll stretch!"

Stretch? It looked like it needed to multiply in order to get around my girth.

I was pretty sure there wasn't enough Crisco in the world to lubricate all of me into *that!* Never one to back down from a challenge though, I headed to the bedroom to give it a shot!

But—before I even attempted "Mission: Impossible"—there were a few things I needed to take care of first. I locked and barricaded the door, pulled down all the window shades, and threw a towel over the camera that monitored my movements 24/7. No one should have to suffer through seeing *THIS* misadventure! There are some things that just can't be *unseen!*

For the first time since I'd entered this competition, I started to feel the sinking sense of looming defeat!

Plopping dejectedly onto the bed beside those tiny "shorts," I had only one thought: *this is IMPOSSIBLE!* But the words of Philippians 4:13 instantly sprang to mind: "I can do ALL things through Christ Who gives me strength!"

I would never have dreamed that particular scripture could apply so beautifully to the challenge of getting into a pair of SPANX! In fact, I felt a little inclined to pray for this poor defenseless pair of unsuspecting SPANX, having no idea of the hurting I was about to put on it!

"Here goes nothing," I said, swallowing my growing apprehension at attempting to stuff all my considerable girth into these little "panties"!

Truthfully, at 283, I would have called them "DRAWZ" instead of "panties"—but I was already down about 80 pounds, so I was up for a new adventure, right?

WRONG!

Staring down my newest nemesis, I slid my foot into the first hole! *It fits! Praise the Lord, it fits!*

My confidence growing, I slid my other foot through the second hole and it also fit nicely!

I've got this, I thought!

I slid them easily over my ankles, everything moving along quite nicely . . . until we came to my *calves*.

Have you *seen* my calves?

They are truly a work of art . . . the best muscles I've got going on this body of mine, bar none. But it's my proud little calves that form the first little "bump in the road!"

Still—a little more stretching and pulling, followed by a good firm tug and they were up, over my calves and climbing higher! Whew . . . I stopped to catch my breath while the poor, defenseless SPANX took a time-out around my knees.

This really hasn't been that bad, I thought. *Maybe Alicia was right . . . anyway, time to keep moving . . .*

So I began the laborious task of tugging this thing up over my thighs, hips, belly, and behind . . .

Moooove to the left.

Moooove to the right.

Hmm . . . this thing was about 20 inches long when I started—so how come it looks like a single strand of twine twisted around my hips?! What's going on here? Why is it wadded up like this and why does it look like belt instead of SPANX? Ugh . . .

I pulled from one side and then the other: no luck! I pulled so hard from the front that my hand slipped and I punched myself in the face! Great . . . now to explain to the producers why I have a fat, bleeding lip. *AWESOME!*

But, looking down to evaluate my progress, I see the weary garment still stuck in a single strand across my hips. *You've got to be kidding!*

I was suddenly struck by a burst of inspiration. *Wait a sec—I'm Asian! Aren't we supposed to be contortionists?!* Inspired, I lunged into a full-out squat—only to find myself lying flat on my bed, on my back, staring up at the ceiling and wondering about the feasibility of installing some sort of pulley system capable of getting these shorts up to my bra line.

Weigh-in is only hours away; not enough time for that . . .

C'mon, Jones—let's go; you can DO this!

After a whole series of shimmies and thrusts, followed by a marathon session of hopping in-place, I had broken out into a "Garmin Zone 4" full-out sweat. But the demonic drawers were no closer to being over my hips and belly!

With some combination of perspiration and prayer, accompanied by a pull powerful enough to have ruptured things I've still not been able to identify, I finally had them over the hump and resting near my navel!

Only 12 more inches to go—if I can just . . . catch . . . my breath . . .

Sitting down on the bed for just a moment to rest, I glanced down. What I saw wasn't pretty!

I couldn't even *SEE* my bottom half *at all,* thanks to the massive mound of flesh protruding out of the top of this contraption! You've heard of muffin top? Yeah, this was more like bursting bakery! It was bad.

It suddenly dawned on me that, if I failed to survive this ordeal, they'd find my body looking like a blown-up button mushroom! That horrifying prospect alone was enough to rouse me back into action!

Gingerly working my way up off the bed, I resumed my regimen of pulling and tugging.

I think I can! I think I can! I think I caaannnnnn!

This was turning into my *fourth* workout for the day!

My heart rate typically climbs to about 150 during a workout; but, glancing at the monitor I was required to wear, I saw that it was at 175 already . . . and still climbing! I think it hit 190 just before I blacked out!

Just kidding. I never actually lost consciousness . . . but it was touch-and-go for a while!

After one final pull, they were *all the way* **up**! *VICTORY!*

Suddenly, I had more questions than answers . . .

How exactly does a person breathe in this thing?

Am I supposed to be seeing spots?

Will they need the "Jaws of Life" to get me out of this monstrosity?

The things one thinks of when stuffed like a sausage into its casing!

Still, I couldn't resist taking a moment to savor my victory! I had defied all the odds and achieved the impossible!

Taking a tentative first step toward the closet to retrieve my tank top (for weigh-in), I suddenly felt something that made me freeze, dead in my tracks.

What was . . . THAT?!

Hold on . . . don't move.

Steady . . . ohh, NOOOO!!!

It's gonna BLOW!

Before I could even get my hand up to grab it, the garment started bunching and then rolling downward with the unstoppable force of Niagara. In a matter of .04 seconds, the SPANX sensed the promised land and rushed all the way back down to my belly button! It all happened so quickly! It's almost as if there was a race happening on my body that no one told me about.

What just happened?! I can't do this again . . . I just CAN'T! I don't have the strength, I don't have the power . . . I just can't do it!

The best way I can describe the force behind this is to ask if you have ever taken a can of biscuits out of the refrigerator? You know how you slowly peel off the outer label, then take your butter knife to gently press on the line . . . ***BOOM! BAM!***

The biscuit can ***EXPLODES!!!*** There is no containing the contents.

That's exactly what happened in my bedroom that morning. The contents could NOT be contained!

Defeated, I looked to see if there was any shrapnel. *Okay there.*

I looked to see if any of my parts had been detached in the explosion. *Whew—everything still intact!*

I looked around to see if anything but my pride had been harmed in the process. Apparently, that was the only casualty.

But I don't want to mislead you or give you the wrong impression. All was not gloom and doom in that room!

Because, no sooner had I popped my own personal can of biscuits, than my entire exposed abdomen burst into the "Hallelujah Chorus" with its first tantalizing taste of returning FREEDOM!

But the euphoria was short-lived . . . as the whole process now had to be repeated. And so it was . . . a mere 15 minutes later I emerged fully clothed and completely exhausted.

We eventually got there, though I had to have help—in the form of reinforcements . . . and *duct tape!*

You think I'm kidding?

Here's a picture to prove it!

Oh . . . the lengths to which vanity will lead us!

Oh . . . the struggle of striving to look thin!

What else could compel a plus-sized woman to force herself into the threads of a toddler?!

That was the day I realized that, **with the Lord's help (and a little duct tape)** . . . *there is NOTHING I can't accomplish.*

And so it is with you, my friend! So it is with you . . .

LESSON #24

BOTH TIGGER *AND* EEYORE CAN HAVE IMPACT.

She was my fiercest (and final) female competitor on the Ranch, but Lori Harrigan-Mack has become one of my dearest friends in the world—despite the fact that we are complete *opposites!*

Were we to inhabit the fanciful world of *Winnie-the-Pooh*, there's no question about it: I would be *Tigger* and Lori would be *Eeyore!*

You remember that drastically different duo, right?

Tigger (the tiger) is best-known for his irrepressible optimism that keeps him literally bouncing through life! ("Bouncing is what Tiggers do best," he says.)

Eeyore (the donkey), on the other hand, is perpetually gloomy and depressed, ever-inclined to fear (and fully *expect*) the worst! ("I was so upset I forgot to be happy" is his observation.)

Without question, I am Tigger and Lori is Eeyore.

I bounce everywhere; she strolls.

I talk a mile a minute; she is very slow to speak.

I'm a cannon; she's more of a long fuse.

Eeyore and Tigger

As I got to know Lori over the course of the competition, I quickly came to understand the sheer folly in daring to ask her anything in the morning . . . until she was at least halfway through her first cup of coffee!

Once she'd reached the halfway point, however, it was ON—as I began to bombard her with questions . . .

"So, Lori—what do you want to do today, huh? Want to hike? Want to jog? Want to swim? Want to go to the gym? What sounds good? Huh? Huh? Huh?"

Lori's reply would inevitably begin with a long sigh.

"Hmm . . . we can go to the gym, I guess."

Once *that* decision was made, I immediately wanted to know what we were going to do once we GOT to the gym . . .

"So, Lori—do you want to start off on the treadmill? Or the elliptical? Or the stationary bike? What do you think? What sounds good? Huh? Huh? Huh?"

Another long sigh.

"Why do you sigh all the time?" I asked (with my characteristic subtlety).

"I didn't even realize I was doing it," she said.

Then, stopping dead in her tracks, she looked at me quizzically and asked: "How do you do it? How do you do this every day? You're always bouncing and happy and have a good attitude about everything! How DO you do it?!"

"Sometimes you just DO," I said. "You just put one foot in front of the other and keep going—because you know it's the right thing!"

She nodded and then we kept going, continuing on to the gym . . . simply because it was the right thing!

When it comes to how we approach life, Lori and I are about as different as night and day. But her journey on *The Biggest Loser* had just as big an impact as mine. In her unique way, she inspired just as many people as I did.

People are just *different.*

We all have different personalities, different strengths and weaknesses, different ways of dealing with life.

But, whatever your personality or perspective, your style and approach will resonate with some people in a way that mine never could. They may look at *me* like I have a third eye—but they will relate to you!

Someone out there needs to hear what you (specifically) have to say (in the way that only you can say it)!

Someone is just waiting to be inspired . . . by YOU!

God can (and will) use you—just the way He's wired you—to make a real impact on those around you . . . because, take it from me, **both Tigger AND Eeyore can have impact.**

LESSON #25

BEAUTY IS *MORE* THAN SKIN DEEP.

Deep down, every woman wants to feel like a princess.

Every woman wants to turn heads and feel beautiful.

The Biggest Loser enabled me to feel like that for the first time in my life.

When I learned that I had made it to "Makeover Week," I was over the moon with excitement!

I mean, what woman wouldn't want to have her hair done by celebrity hairstylist Ken Pavés in his Beverly Hills salon?

With Ken Pavés

Who wouldn't want to have her wardrobe personally selected by legendary fashion consultant Tim Gunn?

Makeover Night – with Tim Gunn and my best friend, Jeni

And pulling up in a limousine and going to an "after party" with Gavin DeGraw—playing a private concert just for me and my friends?

That was easily one of the greatest nights of my life, far exceeding even my wildest expectations—truly the stuff of which dreams are made!

But, believe it or not, the *physical* transformation I underwent during Makeover Week was the LEAST significant of the changes I experienced!

That night was the culmination of a long, arduous process in which: my *hair* was cut, colored, and styled; my *makeup* was done, re-done, and re-touched; my *clothes* were picked out, put on, then fluffed and re-fluffed. Then I was on to my own personal photo shoot with *US Weekly!*

Somebody pinch me . . . 'cuz I *had* to be dreaming!

But it may surprise you to know that the moment of my big "reveal" was the only time in the entire competition when I found myself wanting to run away!

Somewhere—deep inside me—I was feeling something that I had never felt before, and it scared the daylights out of me and made me want to *run!*

You see, for the first time in my entire life, I felt truly *beautiful*—and I had absolutely no idea what to do with that! This was totally new territory for me; I was sailing into uncharted waters . . .

*Makeover Night left me feeling as beautiful
as my stunning trainer!*

But the best part is that, in that moment, I suddenly realized that I didn't feel beautiful just because of what had been done with my hair, makeup, or wardrobe—but because, for the first time in my life, I was catching the tiniest glimpse of what *God* sees in me!

To be sure—I was proud of what all my hard work and dedication had accomplished in enabling me to make it this far in the journey that God had entrusted to me.

But I was most proud of (and simultaneously humbled by) the sudden awareness of how God had *always* seen me—and recognized the truly beautiful woman He had made me to be.

Physical beauty, of course, is widely-admired—but far too little attention is paid to *inner* beauty—which is where a woman really shines!

Don't get me wrong—I will be forever grateful for the experience of Makeover Week. It was something that very few people will ever have a chance to experience (though I would wish it for everyone).

With two equally lovely ladies - Alison Sweeney and Jeni Phelps

But my real makeover happened within.

That, more than anything, is what I wish for YOU!

I want YOU to be able to see yourself the way God does—for only then will you feel truly beautiful, deeply cherished, and extravagantly loved.

You are truly one-of-a-kind . . . whose ***beauty is more*** (far more) ***than skin deep!***

LESSON #26

YOU CAN *ALWAYS* MAKE A COMEBACK!

Where was Bob Harper?

We had just begun production on Season 16 of *The Biggest Loser*. It was our first night of filming, so I had a LOT of questions—but this one rose to the top!

Where WAS Bob Harper?!

For the previous 15 seasons, I'd watched the show religiously—never missing an episode—and Bob Harper, personal trainer to the stars, had been a staple of every single one.

That night, however, when they trotted out all the trainers (including a couple of newbies I'd never even *heard* of), there was NO Bob Harper!

From where I was standing, *The Biggest Loser* without Bob Harper seemed like peanut butter without jelly—which meant that I was trying not to choke . . . on this, my *second* major disappointment of this new season.

The *first* was the unprecedented sequestration to which we were being subjected!

I knew (from previous seasons) that contestants were *always* given the opportunity to communicate with their families back home—usually pretty early in the process. I'd counted on that, convincing myself (and my family) that this wouldn't be so bad—since at least we'd be able to stay in touch.

So you can imagine my surprise (and displeasure) when I got to the Ranch and discovered that we were allowed no communication with family or friends at all—no phone calls or letters or anything for weeks!

In fact, we were completely cut off from the outside world; we couldn't even go to the store to buy our own underwear or personal products! (Do you have any idea how difficult it is to explain the different types of tampons—and why it matters—to a male production assistant?!)

To be honest, the complete lack of communication was probably the most difficult element of our season—particularly for the moms in the group. The inability to have any contact with their kids created a tremendous amount of tension on set in those early weeks.

To make matters worse, we were given absolutely no explanation for the isolation, but left to wonder at the reasons for this unprecedented blackout!

It wasn't until Week 16 that I discovered the answer . . . and both of my disappointments were suddenly resolved!

Turns out that Bob Harper was indeed still on the show—but the producers had cut off all contact with our friends and family so that none would slip and let us in on the secret of his "Comeback Canyon"!

With "Crazy Bob" Harper

You see—the particular innovation of our season was that, unbeknownst to us, whenever a contestant was eliminated from the show, they weren't sent home (as had previously always been the case). Instead, they were taken about 10 miles away to a secret location known as "Comeback Canyon." There, they were given a second chance: an opportunity to train with Bob Harper and make a comeback!

I can't even tell you how much I love that concept!

All of our contestants were former athletes who had come on the show trying to earn a second chance. Even after falling short there, they would be given yet *another* chance. That is such a perfect picture of the grace of God Who, regardless of past performance, stands ever ready to offer another chance! (Just make sure you seize it when it comes!)

Life doesn't always turn out like you hope it will. It can be full of disappointments and setbacks.

Yet hope remains.

Your *past* does not have to define your *future!*

God may have closed certain doors in your life . . . to encourage you to move in another direction (one that He knows will ultimately prove far better than the one you were determined to take).

You may feel so overwhelmed by your past that your future seems hopeless, but I urge you to forget the past and look to the One Who can bring you back from anything!

Don't give up on your hopes and dreams! The further you've fallen, the better positioned you are for the greatest comeback ever!

So what are you waiting for? You're in position for the WIN; now go get it!

No matter what has gone before, with *His* enabling, ***you can always make a comeback!***

LESSON #27

GOD HAS MORE IN STORE THAN YOU CAN IMAGINE!

My journey on *The Biggest Loser* was certainly not without its share of disappointments (the finale being a biggie). All along the way, however, the Lord sent me little surprises to encourage me and keep me going.

He saved some especially nice surprises for my birthday . . .

It was an unusually beautiful autumn afternoon and I was enjoying a walk with my trainer when, all of a sudden, Jen turned to me and said, "So—you have a pretty big birthday coming up!"

"Turning the Big 4-0 this Sunday," I acknowledged, not wanting to admit that this particular milestone had already caused me more *anxiety* than *anticipation*.

Still, if one HAS to turn 40, I couldn't imagine a better place to do it than the Ranch . . . or a better group of people to do it with than my coach and fellow contestants!

"I know you're a long way from home," Jen continued, "but we want to find a way to make this day special for you. So let me ask you this: is there anything specific that you would really like to DO for your birthday?"

One thing sprang immediately to mind.

"Actually, there is," I said. "There's this church in LA that's been on my 'bucket list' to visit and, since my birthday's gonna be on a Sunday, I can't think of *anything* I'd rather do than THAT!"

From the moment we entered Hillsong Church,
it felt like HOME!

"Let me see what I can work out," she said, whipping out her phone and immediately beginning to text "the powers that be"—who quickly signaled their approval, clearing her to take me . . . and anyone else who wanted to go!

To a degree I could never have imagined, God was about go "above and beyond"—using my 40th birthday to show me just how very precious I am to Him!

As Sunday morning dawned, I started the day with my usual "prayer walk" around the Ranch—carefully explaining to God that, as excited as I was to be going to church that day, I had every intention of keeping it "cool."

You see, I'm typically a pretty dynamic worshipper—lifting my hands high in the air and singing loudly and with exuberance. But the last thing I wanted to do on this day was to make those who were going to be joining me uncomfortable.

Of course, I had no sooner gotten my carefully-constructed "explanation" out of my mouth than I sensed the Lord saying to my spirit: "Look, Jones—I want you to worship exactly the way I *created* you to worship . . . which is with your whole heart!"

I quietly agreed to try . . .

A few hours later, five of us arrived at Hillsong Church for what turned out to be one of the most tremendous worship experiences of my life!

With my crew at church . . . on one of the most
unforgettable days of my life!

I could tell my friends were somewhat taken aback by
the unanticipated abandon with which many were able
to worship that morning and one even confessed, in
slack-jawed amazement, that she'd never seen anything
like *that* before!

My heart sank a little at the announcement of a guest
speaker . . . until they revealed his name. Pastor Brian
Houston—whom I had long admired and wanted to
hear—had come all the way from Sydney, Australia to
be there that morning! What a sweet surprise! Instantly,
I knew that this was another of God's birthday gifts,
picked out just especially for me!

Pastor Brian wrapped up his message with a stirring call to salvation; and, in the single greatest joy of my entire *Biggest Loser* journey, I got to see some of my new friends join many others in the congregation in responding to that call!

The prospect of one day spending all eternity with these who had become so dear to me was, by far, the greatest birthday gift I could ever have received. It was a moment that I will remember for as long as I live (and then some)!

My heart was full as we left the service, and Jen treated us to sushi at one of her favorite places before returning us to the Ranch.

The minute we got back, I changed into my workout gear and hit the treadmill, having no idea that I had yet *another* birthday surprise on the way . . .

Engrossed in my workout, I barely noticed the sound of a door opening behind me . . . until I heard a deep male voice singing "Happy Birthday" to ME!

I turned to see Dolvett Quince serenading me in song! What a moment *that* was!

But the moment was not yet over when my disbelieving ears heard him say, "Sonya, I've got a little birthday surprise for you. The Masi is right downstairs if you'd like to take her for a spin!"

Wait—*did Dolvett Quince just offer to let me drive his Maserati through the hills of Malibu for my 40th birthday?!* I must be God's favorite today, for sure! This was more than I could have anticipated. So off we went . . . with me at the wheel and Dolvett in the passenger seat. What a day!

Behind the wheel of Dolvett's Maserati

The Bible says that God "is able to do immeasurably more than all we ask or imagine, according to His power that is at work within us" (Ephesians 3:20). I have found that to be true over and over again.

God is able to do more than you can even *imagine*. I know that's saying a lot but, if you can *dream* it, He can *exceed* it!

He will blow your mind with His blessings!

I can't tell you how many times I've experienced that in my life; my 40th birthday was just the "icing on the cake" (pun intended)!

Trust me: **God has more in store**—for YOU—*than you can* possibly *imagine!*

LESSON #28

ALWAYS LISTEN TO WISE COUNSEL.

The Biggest Loser: Season 16 was rapidly coming to a close, and we were down to the final four contestants.

In just 48 hours, we would be leaving the "safety" of the Ranch and heading for home—and I was scared out of my mind!

Don't get me wrong—I was excited about seeing my friends and family, but more than a little apprehensive about my ability to continue dropping weight on my own . . . as I would *have* to do to have any hope of winning the Grand Prize! (I didn't even want to *think* about all the former contestants who'd put their weight right back on!)

Just before we left for home, Executive Producer Joel Relampagos sat us down for a pointed conversation. From Day One, Joel had always seemed to genuinely care about us—not just as *contestants*, but as *people*—so I really took his words to heart.

With our amazing Executive Producer,
Joel Relampagos

"As you prepare to walk out these doors," he said, "I just want you to know that, for you, the world will never be the same—because millions of people now know who you are."

"I want you to remember that, every week, these millions of people invite you into their living rooms. You may not know them, but they *feel* like they know you!

"They have taken joy in your journey and feel like you are part of their family—so remember that as you pass these people at the airport and in the grocery store!"

Two days later, I was walking through the LA airport when, for the first time, I was recognized by a complete stranger. Instantly, Joel's words echoed in my mind. *You may not know them, but they feel like they know you.*

Joel's wise counsel ensured that I would remember to honor the millions who had taken this incredible journey with me. As a result, to this day, I have never turned down any request for a picture or an autograph.

As I mentioned in Chapter Three, one of my education professors had offered some similarly sage advice on my last day of class at Greenville University in 1996 . . .

"Ladies and gentlemen," he said, "may I remind you that you don't determine whether or not you are going to be a role model; you simply determine what *type* of role model you will be."

Wise words from two wise men.

You will be remembered—more than anything else—for how you treat other people.

How are YOU going to treat the people with whom you come in contact?

Are you going to be a *positive* role model . . . or a *poor* one?

The choice is yours.

I am unspeakably grateful for all those who have spoken wisdom into my life, and urge you to look for—and *listen* to—the same!

Take it from me—you should ***always listen to wise counsel!***

LESSON #29

STEER CLEAR OF VICIOUS CYCLES.

Getting back home to train for the Finale proved to be everything I had anticipated and then some. It was equal parts exhilarating and exhausting, stimulating and stressful, fulfilling and frightening!

On the positive side, the support I found from my friends and family back home went far beyond anything I could have imagined. It felt like the entire community had my back!

While still on the Ranch (once our sequestration had been lifted), I received letter after letter from back home—all saying: "Sonya, you have no idea how big this thing has gotten around here! People are so excited!"

They were right.

I came off the plane to people wearing t-shirts with my name on them and my face plastered on signs all over town! The level of support I received surpassed that of my wildest dreams!

That was the *great* part—but there was a *grueling* part, as well . . .

I had to work out practically every waking hour—beginning with my *first* 5k of the day every morning at 5:44 A.M. and ending 15 hours later with an intense training session in the gym (after a *second* and third 5k sandwiched in-between)!

This was all in addition to working my regular full-time job, co-teaching 27 classes to some 500 students—not to mention still having to *make* time to EAT and *find* time to SLEEP!

Needless to say, there was virtually no time left for any real social life. It would have been a great time to BE Sonya Jones—had it not been so grueling that I could scarcely remember that I WAS Sonya Jones! I was doing well to remember my name; this girl was exhausted!

In addition to the exercise regimen, of course, I had to maintain iron discipline and a laser-like focus on my diet—none of this "just grab something on the go" stuff!

On the one hand, I felt ready to take on the world—but, as the stress mounted, I also found myself needing and wanting to eat more. Not just *more;* I was increasingly drawn to unhealthy choices and began battling the urge to binge (which, of course, is what had landed me on *The Biggest Loser* to begin with).

Fast-food restaurants and donut shops proved to be growing sources of temptation, along with the greatest culprit of all: the gas station/convenience store!

Unfortunately, there was no way to avoid temptation altogether. I still had to get *gas* and *groceries,* after all!

I'll never forget one particular night when, at the end of a long and exhausting day, I was heading home from the gym and needed to stop off at the grocery store to pick up some fruit and veggies.

Moving to the produce section, I had to pass by the bakery area . . . where my eye immediately fell on an unnaturally outsized piece of white cake with buttercream icing (beautifully encased in a crystal-clear container to showcase its considerable charms)!

Averting my gaze, I proceeded straight to the fruit and veggies as planned, then started for the checkout.

That's when I heard it . . .

"Sonya . . . Sonya . . ."

That *cake* was calling my name (which *it* remembered even if *I* didn't)!

"Sonya . . . don't forget about ME! It's been so long. I miss you! Let's be friends again . . ."

Initially, I walked right on past the bakery and made it halfway to the checkout . . . before I turned around; telling myself that I had to at least go check out those cries and make sure everyone back there was okay!

Whatever you need to tell yourself, right?

In that moment, I felt powerless to resist those voices. The urge to head toward the bakery was more than I could handle. But I'm sure you don't need me to tell you that, once I got back to the bakery area, it was OVER!

With one swift, stealthy motion, I picked up that piece of cake and shoved it under my veggies (where no prying eyes would be the wiser) and headed for the checkout. The *self*-checkout, of course—as I certainly didn't want anyone to SEE me with this cake!

Still, just to be on the safe side, I rehearsed my cleverly-concocted cover story: I was just picking this up for a friend!

Careful to bag the cake separately from my fruit and veggies, once I was safely through the self-check, I swung by the service desk just long enough to ask if I could leave my bag there while I stopped off to use the restroom.

You see where this is going, don't you?

Walking into this public restroom, I lowered myself onto the stool and lovingly removed that piece of cake from its hiding place in the bag.

I couldn't free it from that plastic container fast enough as, with my bare hands, I greedily consumed every last bite . . . all while sitting on a disgusting public toilet!

In that moment, I suddenly flashed back to the Ranch and flooded with shame as I remembered the parting words of our producers: "When you get home, make sure you connect with a good counselor."

Who has time for that? I'd thought. *I'll be too busy training for Finale! Besides, I don't need to see any counselor! I've GOT this!*

But clearly IT had ME!

I was caught in the throes of addiction, enslaved just as much as any drug addict—even if my drug did happen to come disguised in the form of food!

You'd better bet I took pains to dispose of any and every trace of potentially incriminating evidence—just as I looked both ways when exiting both the stall and the restroom itself, just to make sure I hadn't been seen.

My addiction was proving to be a wicked and vicious cycle.

In the end, it would take the help of a professional counselor to get me off that cycle (more on that in Chapter 35)—but there are certainly things I could have done that night to avoid getting ON the cycle in the first place.

I might have been honest with others about the struggle I was having and enlisted their help in praying against temptation, while asking them to hold me accountable.

Failing that, I might at least have asked my roommate to make the grocery run instead.

I *could* have done any number of things, but I didn't—and, in the end, it was a lot harder getting *off* that cycle than it would have been had I never gone anywhere *near* it.

I'm still not proud of what I did that night, but I share this story in hopes that it will encourage YOU to be careful and ***steer clear of vicious cycles.***

LESSON #30

NEVER IGNORE WARNING SIGNS!

Because I was so busy training for Finale once I got home—totally focused on winning the prize—I almost never allowed time for any real *social* interaction.

One Friday night, however, I made a rare exception to go out to dinner with friends at a swanky new restaurant downtown.

In hindsight, I should have stayed at the gym.

Downtown parking on a busy Friday night can be murder even under the best of circumstances; and, sure enough, we ended up having to park several blocks away from the restaurant.

Once we entered its doors, however, all was forgotten!

The restaurant was located in a gorgeous old building—featuring full-length, ceiling-to-floor windows across all sides. It had tremendous character and had been beautifully re-purposed—so much so that I was suddenly re-thinking my outfit, wondering if perhaps I should have dressed up a bit more.

Still, I was wearing a nice shirt and a pair of jeans—all carefully designed to conceal my ever-present SPANX shorts.

For those of you who aren't familiar with SPANX, I hate you—at least I really *want* to, but Jesus won't let me. So I guess maybe I should just explain the concept instead.

SPANX is a brand of compression garment that does wonders to "hide a multitude of sins"—firming things up and making you appear a whole lot thinner than you actually are. As a result, they had become my new best friend and the bane of my existence—all at the same time!

This particular pair was in the form of high-waisted shorts that extended from the top of my knee all the way up to my bra line (in order to smooth over all of those not-so-smooth parts in-between). They weren't always the most comfortable things in the world—since they are, of necessity, a bit *constricting*. By this time, however, I was quite used to them and determined to let nothing mar my enjoyment of what promised to be a great evening!

Dinner was lovely: fabulous food and even finer conversation, punctuated by a lot of laughs! The time passed all-too-quickly until I realized that it was getting late, and I still needed to get to the gym for my evening workout.

Just as I was paying the bill, I glanced out the establishment's enormous glass front to see that the sky had opened and it was POURING! (I'm talking "flash-flood" material; you couldn't even see across the street for the rain!)

Reasoning that I was both the *driver* and the fastest *runner* in the group, I offered to run the several blocks required to retrieve the car. No one tried to stop me, so I set off on my sure-to-be-soggy sprint . . .

I had gotten no more than 50 feet, however, when I was struck by a sudden chill and felt like I was slogging through a mud field! *What in tarnation . . . ?!*

Now, I'm no *endurance* runner, but a mere 50 feet should be no great challenge—nor should this *concrete* sidewalk feel like a *mud* field!

Casting a glance to my right, I suddenly found myself looking straight into the glass front of the restaurant . . . with a sea of wide-eyed (open-mouthed) patrons staring back at me!

That's when I realized that they were not looking me in the *eye,* but focused on parts a bit further *south.*

Following their gaze downward, I discovered to my horror that my jeans were inexplicably bunched down around my ankles!

Apparently, my SPANX had prevented me from sensing their slippage on the way down—so a whole lot of people

were interrupting their meal for the unscripted enter-
tainment of watching a still-generously-proportioned
woman bolting down the sidewalk, fully-exposed in
a pair of nude-colored SPANX shorts! *Great food . . .
AND a free show!*

What's a girl to DO in that moment?

This girl did the only thing she could. I waved with all
the cheerfulness I could muster, while simultaneously
pulling up my pants and gallantly continuing on my
gallop to get the car—all in one fell swoop!

My brave (game) face notwithstanding, it's difficult to
overstate my mortification.

Ever since I'd gotten back from California, people all
over my hometown had been trying to catch a glimpse
of me—and I'd just given them more of a glimpse than
ANY of us bargained for!

When I finally got home that night, I turned on the
news with fear and trembling—bracing myself for any
breaking story about *"police searching for Biggest Loser
who flashed downtown diners!"*

I should have paid attention to the sudden *cold*.

I should at least have made a mental note when mis-
taking *concrete* for *mud*.

Speaking of mental notes, I'm making one now: never
leave the house without a belt . . . and never, under
any circumstance, wear nude-colored SPANX shorts

if there's even the slightest chance I may be dropping my drawers in a public place!

Warning signs are there for a reason.

All I can say, folks, is be vigilant. Make sure you're aware of your surroundings—and *never*, ever *ignore warning signs!*

LESSON #31

SOME DAYS YOU'RE THE BUG;
SOME DAYS YOU'RE THE WINDSHIELD.

January 29, 2015. The Finale was finally here!

I stood there on stage, poised to pick up my check for $250,000 . . .

BOOM! The confetti was falling . . . but it wasn't for *me!*

I *lost* the competition.

I was CERTAIN I was going to win!

In fact, if you had told me 30 minutes beforehand that I was going to lose, I would have told you that you were crazy! There was no way I could lose!

After all, I'd done absolutely everything RIGHT!

I ate right and exercised faithfully, adhering religiously to the diet and fitness routines prescribed for me—even *sleeping* according to schedule!

I did everything that I was told to do in precisely the way I'd been told to do it! I honestly don't know of anything that I could have done any differently.

I can't tell you how many people have come up to me since and said, "Betcha wish you had gone to the bathroom one last time right before you got on that scale that night, huh!"

Duh! Do you honestly think that never occurred to me? I *did* go!

I was just SURE I was going to win—especially since I felt like I was *supposed* to win!

I'd maintained my place as the "Biggest Loser" for the last 13 weeks on the Ranch and was heavily *favored* to win!

I just *knew* that prize was mine . . . until I watched them hand it to *Toma!*

Hard as it was, while the confetti was still falling, I rushed right over to him to offer my congratulations. And, truthfully, if I had to lose to someone, I wouldn't have wanted it to be anyone else.

We started together and remained on the same team together for the entire competition—constantly pushing and encouraging each other (as the other's biggest fan)—and now we were ending together. He just narrowly edged me out.

But I couldn't have lost to a nicer guy! He was a worthy competitor who had earned my deepest respect and admiration.

As I say, if I had to lose to someone, I was glad that it was to *him*.

But the truth is: I *HATE* to lose . . . and have never done it very well!

Yet, the minute Toma's name was announced, I knew what I had to do . . .

Standing there under the heat of the lights, I remembered that there were millions of little eyes fixed on me in that moment—watching, wondering, waiting to see how I was going to react to defeat.

This wasn't just the loss of a game, mind you. This was a loss of a quarter of a million dollars in front of five million people on national television! This was a BIG one! A tough pill to swallow when you've wanted something so badly and worked so hard to attain it . . .

But for my entire professional life as a teacher and coach, I had drilled into my students that "it's not whether you win or lose, but how you play the game!"

Again and again, I had told them:

- *It's okay if you don't always come out on top—as long as you give it your all.*

- *Winning isn't everything.*

- *As long as you don't beat yourself, you can still be proud of your accomplishments.*

Now it was time to put my money where my mouth was—and give Toma his due!

I knew that a lot of those little eyes watching me that night were also incredibly disappointed. Not disappointed IN me, but disappointed FOR me.

Heck, bravely as I tried to cover it, *I* was disappointed too!

Practicing what I'd always preached was probably harder in that moment than at any other time in my life—but I knew that I was running in (and training others for) a much *bigger* race . . .

In the end, amid a flood of conflicting emotions, there was peace—as I forced myself to remember . . . not just who I *am*, but Whom I *represent*.

As a follower of Christ (who claims to trust Him to lead my life and to order my steps), I have to understand that He knew about this long before it ever happened. He asks me to trust Him in both good times and bad . . . and, truthfully, every life will know a lot of both!

You may eat right and exercise religiously . . . and still get cancer.

You may be the "perfect" kid—who makes good grades and never gets in trouble . . . but mom and dad still divorce.

You can be the best employee in the world . . . but the company still closes and you lose your job anyway.

Sometimes the chips just don't fall your way.

The chips didn't fall my way that night . . . at least not the way I'd *hoped* they would.

But, in that moment, I chose to trust that there was a higher purpose at work and that God had a bigger plan for my life than that of winning the title of *The Biggest Loser.*

In that moment, I realized that I really *did* believe that—to my deepest core!

I still do.

With Toma and Jen just moments after my loss.
I was able to smile because I was genuinely happy for him.

That's why, looking back, I wouldn't change a thing.

Sure, it would have been nice not to have a mortgage payment or to be able to take my friends and family on a vacation they would never forget.

But I gained something that night that money can't buy—not even a quarter of a million dollars!

I was able to show the world (and show myself) that you really CAN look defeat in the eye and rise above it—because, at the end of the day, it ultimately *isn't* whether you win or lose, but how you play the game!

I still believe—now more than ever—that God has a plan and a purpose for every life (*yours* as well as *mine*) that FAR exceeds anything you or I could ever imagine!

So here's the bottom line: ***some days you're the bug and some days you're the windshield . . .***

But every day, He is *faithful*—and His plans for YOU are *good!*

LESSON #32

PUT YOUR EMPHASIS IN THE RIGHT PLACE.

It's all about where you place your emphasis!

My season on *The Biggest Loser* was entitled: "Glory Days"—because all of the contestants that year, myself included, were former athletes trying to regain those "Glory Days" gone by . . . when we'd been in a LOT better shape!

Now—some of us, myself included, were fairly *average* athletes, to be honest, but there were some real show-stoppers on the cast, as well!

- A two-time Super Bowl champion *(Damien Woody)*

- A three-time gold medalist in women's fastpitch softball *(Lori Harrigan-Mack)*

- A tennis gold medalist and Wimbledon run-ner-up *(Zina Garrison)*

- An NFL quarterback for 12 seasons *(Scott Mitchell)*

- A star player with the WNBA *(Vanessa Hayden)*

These were not just your average, run-of-the-mill ath-letes . . . they were STUDS! Men and women whom I not only admired, but idolized!

And then, there was . . . *me.*

Sonya Jones—a two-time All-American fastpitch soft-ball player from a tiny little NCAA Division Three college in Greenville, Illinois.

Needless to say, I was not exactly the star athlete on that cast.

It took me about 13 weeks to stop seeing myself as the underdog and begin to believe that I really could compete with this amazing group!

Eventually, however, a little three-word phrase became my defining motto and driving mantra . . .

Why not ME?

Day after day, that phrase began to drive me—giving me the push I needed to win the competition . . .

When I didn't feel like running my 22nd mile of the day . . .

Why not ME?

When I didn't feel like doing my fourth set of 44 burpees . . .

Why not ME?

When I didn't feel like sprinting up the mountain for the eighth time . . .

Why not ME?

When I felt like eating more than my allotted calories, it was that question that helped keep me in check!

Those three little words continually pushed me to do everything I possibly could to win that competition—and, truthfully, I knew that I was going to win!

There was not a doubt in my mind.

You see, by the end of the season, I had been the biggest loser on the Ranch for 13 weeks in a row.

I'd had the highest percentage of weight loss of any contestant on the show since Week Five.

I *knew* that I was going to win.

WHY NOT ME?

Fast-forward to my finale night . . .

I stood on-stage at *The Biggest Loser* finale and listened as they announced Toma as the winner!

I lost the title of "The Biggest Loser" by .01% of my body weight (the closest margin-of-loss in *Biggest Loser* history).

I lost $250,000 by less than a pound! (You can make your checks payable to "Sonya Jones" and that's "Sonya" with a "y.")

I *LOST* the competition.

In all the hoopla and hubbub of that moment, there was no opportunity for the hurt to sink in . . . until I fell into bed that night.

Finally, as I lay in bed at 3 A.M. with the lights out, hot tears began to roll . . .

All of a sudden—those three little words that for months had driven me to be the *victor* now made me a *victim*—as, instantly, "Why not ME?" morphed into "Why NOT me?!"

A statement of drive was suddenly transformed into a statement of defeat . . .

Why NOT me? *I had done everything right . . .*

Why NOT me? *I had bathed the entire competition (from start to finish) in prayer . . .*

Why NOT me? *I'd given God the glory every step of the way . . .*

Same words. Different emphasis. Totally different meaning.

I lay there in bed for a couple of hours, wrestling with my emotions, before the fog started to lift and a different perspective began to emerge . . .

All of a sudden, it dawned on me that, while I had not won the title I'd sought (or the quarter of a million dollars that went with it) and was not, at that moment, on the red eye to New York City to be on *The Today Show* and *Live with Kelly and Michael* (which, truthfully, hurt more than anything) . . . I *had* WON!

I had won my *life* and my *health!* I'm no longer on a bunch of medicines, but am at a healthy weight—and starting to *love* the person that God created!

So as I lay there in bed that night, my emphasis shifted once again . . .

Why not *me?*

Why not *me* . . . to see what God has in store next?

Why not *me* . . . to use this tremendous experience I've been given to impact the lives of others?

Why not *me* . . . to "pay forward" all the lessons I learned on the show— since not everyone will have that same opportunity?

Why not ME?

Same words, different *emphasis* . . . different *meaning!*

So be sure to always **put your *emphasis* in the right place.**

It can make the difference in your being a *victim* . . . or *victor!*

Why not YOU?

Why not YOU . . . to see what God has in store next?

Why not YOU . . . to use *your* life experiences to impact others?

Why not YOU . . . to pay forward all of the amazing lessons that *you* have learned through *your* life experiences?

Why not YOU?

Best Makeover Night EVER

Fun times . . . before the dreaded weigh-in!

Happy Birthday to ME!

I think I enjoyed this challenge a lot more than Rob did!

In the gym with Bob Harper

In Vegas all gussied up and ready to go

Introducing Jeni and Jessie on Makeover Night

Ken Pavés getting ready to work his magic . . .

Lori and Rondalee were two of my best friends on the show

Lori, Jen, and I forged a very special bond

One of the best surprises of Makeover Week –
discovering that they'd flown in Jeni!

Quite a transformation for Toma and me!

The gang in Vegas

The only two girls to survive until Makeover Week

The White Team with football legend (and Super Bowl champ) Donald Driver

Those heels about killed me

What a great group of people!

What an honor to be coached by one of the greats –
NFL legend Donald Driver himself!

With Tim Gunn during Makeover Week

Yep folks, that's MUD!

LESSON #33

THERE IS POWER IN ACCOUNTABILITY.

There is real power in accountability.

I discovered that firsthand soon after returning home from the show—as people from all over everywhere were holding me accountable in all sorts of ways. Some of them I appreciated; some . . . well, not so much.

Take the fan who came up to my table when I sat down for dinner at a local steak house. "Do you mind if I just stand here to see what you order?" she asked. *Sure—because that's not at all intrusive!*

On another occasion, I was out purchasing supplies for a friend's birthday party when a fellow shopper pulled alongside me, warily eyeing my cart full of chips and sweets (typical party fare, in other words). "Aren't you afraid that you'll put your weight back on by eating all that stuff?" she asked. *Well, maybe . . . if I planned on eating this entire sheet cake, five bags of chips, and economy-sized container of party peanuts by myself—in which case, I'll keep you posted!*

Of course, most people really mean well—so I tried constantly to remind myself that, in their own way, they were invested in my *Biggest Loser* journey themselves. Some of them seemed almost as excited about it as I was!

Most were simply trying to be helpful and encouraging, as they genuinely did not want to see me put back on all the weight I'd fought so hard to lose. I couldn't help but appreciate that!

And, to be perfectly honest, I signed up for this the minute I agreed to go on national television as a contestant on a popular reality TV show. If I didn't always appreciate the attention (or scrutiny), I had no one to blame but myself.

Now that I'm a few years removed from the show, it's easier to see how the involuntary accountability which I experienced was both helpful and hurtful.

On the one hand, I'm still grateful that people cared enough to check in. On the other, I've come to recognize that this sometimes had the unintended effect of moving me even deeper into addiction.

For instance, because I didn't want people to see me eating unhealthy things in public, I was always careful to eat well in front of others. Yet watching them eat the junk which I had always been so fond of only whetted a renewed desire for it myself. That was a desire that, ultimately, I could not quench.

As a result, I would get up from the healthy meal I'd enjoyed for public consumption . . . only to stop at a gas station and consume 4 or 5 donuts on the way home (disposing of all the wrappers, of course—so that no one was the wiser).

In that way, I eventually learned to navigate my way around various levels of "accountability."

To be fair, I never wanted to let anyone down—least of all those who had been so faithful to walk that road *with* me.

But, for the first time in my life, I really didn't want to let *myself* down either.

I truly wanted to stay the course toward a healthier, happier life! I wanted to be an inspiration to others—by assuring them that, if *I* could get healthy, then there was no reason in the world that *they* couldn't!

Though accountability wasn't always fun, it ultimately proved more helpful than I can say. Countless people prepared nutritious and healthy meals for me, so that I wouldn't have to spend time cooking. I was blessed with a running buddy—who faithfully showed up at my door every single morning (at precisely 5:44 A.M.) to make sure I was up and ready to go on the first 5K of the day. Rain or shine, she was right there by my side every step of the way—giving me just the push I needed to keep on putting one foot in front of the other.

The reality is that accountability can be a tremendous tool . . . if you'll let it remind you that people aren't just being nosy, but really do *care* and genuinely want to see (and help) you succeed!

The bottom line is this: it's not always comfortable; in fact, it *rarely* is. But, if you're willing to submit to it, ***there is*** real ***power in accountability!***

LESSON #34

EXPECT THE UNEXPECTED.

I often think back to one particular afternoon on the Ranch . . .

I was running the mile when that beautiful trainer, Jessie Pavelka, appeared from out of nowhere and came up alongside me!

"Hey, Sonya!" he said. "Can I talk to you for a minute?"

"Really, Jessie?" I responded. "Can it wait? I'm right in the middle of my run!" *I mean, it's not like he had his shirt off or anything—or, let me tell you, I'd have been stopped in my tracks!*

"C'mon, Sonya!" he persisted. "Just give me a minute, okay? Please?"

How could I argue with *that?!* I couldn't—so motioned for him to continue.

"Listen," he said, "when you get home, you're going to need to get a good agent."

"An agent?" I asked. "What on earth do I need with an agent?!"

I couldn't believe my ears when I heard his answer.

"You're gonna need a good agent who can help you manage all your speaking engagements."

Speaking engagements? ME?!

That's the last thing in the world I had ever thought about!

You've got to understand—I'd had a pretty severe speech impediment growing up. I stuttered and stammered my way all through elementary, high school, and college, even taking special classes to try to curb the problem (with limited success, I might add).

Thankfully, I no longer got made fun of as much as I had as a kid, but my stuttering was something that I remained very self-conscious of, even as an adult.

"You have a lot of great things to say," Jessie continued, "and a great way of saying them! Every week, when you get up there on that scale, we're all waiting in eager anticipation of what you're going to say! I don't think you realize just how inspiring you are! I'm telling you, when you get home, you're gonna need a good agent."

I was convinced he'd been out in the hot sun too long; clearly, he was getting overheated and it was affecting his brain. *If only he'd take that shirt off and cool down . . .*

"Jessie," I said, finally managing to get a grip on myself, "I appreciate that, but I really don't think that's something I'm ever going to have to worry about!" *Now, unless you plan to take that shirt off, I'm going to get on with my run . . .*

"Trust me, Sonya, you're going to need someone to help you once you're off the show."

He trailed off at that point, but I continued to think about what he had said.

With Jessie Pavelka - whose encouraging words helped put me on a path I'd never imagined

He had a point—if only in that, to my great surprise, I had discovered that, when I stepped up on the scale, I relished the opportunity to share my heart and speak the words I knew the Lord was giving me. To be honest, that caught me completely off-guard . . . because I had NEVER enjoyed speaking in front of people!

Even so, I was no dietician or trainer or expert on diet or fitness (or anything else, for that matter)—so I was pretty sure that, once I stepped off the Ranch, no one was going to care what I had to say.

But I was wrong.

I had completely failed to anticipate the platform my experience on the show had created for me, complete with a built-in audience! I'd no sooner gotten home than the invitations to speak started pouring in . . . from all over the country!

Pretty soon, I was speaking in schools, churches, hospitals, races, corporate events—you name it!

I still had my full-time job as a teacher and coach Monday through Friday, but nearly every weekend I was living out of a suitcase as I jetted across the country just trying to keep up with the demands of a calendar that was suddenly FULL of speaking engagements!

I couldn't believe it—but what I found even harder to believe was how much I *loved* it! I was having the time of my life out there!

Teaching and coaching remained my first love, of course. With two master's degrees in education, I truly loved the field. Even after all my years in teaching, I continued to wake up every morning, thinking: "I *get* to go to work today!" I had never been able to imagine myself doing anything *else.*

By the end of 2015, however, right after returning from an extended speaking tour in California, I found myself saying: "I would never leave education . . . *unless* someone wants to pay me for full-time public speaking" (words I never thought would come out of MY mouth)!

You see, somewhere along the way, I'd fallen in love. (Not exactly the kind of love I'd left the show *hoping* to find, but hey—we take what we can get, right?)

I had fallen in love with the power of a positive message married to a microphone!

We are inundated with negative messages already—so, when I stumbled onto the power of *positivity* to turn back that tide and hold out hope to those in desperate need of it, I was hooked!

I was head over heels with the opportunity to stand up in front of a room full of people—looking them in the eye and watching their whole countenance and outlook change—as I reassured them . . .

You're worth it!

You matter!

You are deeply loved!

> *Trust me—if I can make a change, then you certainly can!*

I could never have imagined finding something new that I would become so passionate about in my 40th year of life, but the thrill of helping people and offering them hope proved contagious!

I wasn't entirely sure what to DO with all that; but when the opportunity came to become part of the John Maxwell Team, I jumped at it. I became a certified speaker, seizing every platform I could find—as I continued, every single day, to pray: "Lord, just order my steps."

Because of His leading, however, I actually turned down quite a few job offers and product endorsement requests. I was determined not to attach my name to anything that I didn't believe in 100%!

Then—in January of 2016—I was approached by Hospital Sisters Health System (HSHS), one of the fastest growing medical groups in the country, asking me to join their team.

Based in central and southern Illinois, HSHS Medical Group offered me a position as an outreach representative—partnering with them to promote health and wellness in the community by simply combining my story with theirs . . . as a *full-time public speaker!*

Reluctant as I was to leave the classroom, the more I learned about this group (particularly their commitment to treating people with respect, care, competence, and joy—in the name of Jesus), the more convinced I was that this was a once-in-a-lifetime opportunity the Lord was sending my way! From that point forward, I was *ALL-IN!*

As Providence would have it, I began the process of closing the door on the classroom by signing a contract with HSHS Medical Group on the first anniversary of my *Biggest Loser* finale—January 29, 2016—exactly one year later, to the day!

Doing what I love best - empowering others
(for HSHS Medical Group)

I'll be honest: I still miss seeing my kids every day and the deep involvement in my athletes' lives (and probably always will). But I am absolutely blown away by how much I *love* what I'm doing NOW. I am still the person who says, "I *get* to go to work today!"

This change in career is something I would never have anticipated!

Come to think of it, I could say that about a LOT of things . . .

I would never have anticipated:

- Becoming a contestant on *The Biggest Loser*

- Falling in love with public speaking

- Leaving my job for a whole new career with an organization that I have grown to love and respect

I never expected *any* of the blessings I have received—but GOD . . . !

He really DOES have more in store for *all* of us—and that means YOU too—than *any* of us could ever ask or imagine!

So make sure you keep Him first.

Then ask Him to order your steps.

Be sure to follow His lead.

But I'm telling you now: ***expect the unexpected!***

LESSON #35

COUNSELING ISN'T JUST FOR WEIRDOS . . .
IS IT?

One of the toughest things to deal with when I came home from the show was that, while I looked like a completely different person on the outside, all of my internal struggles remained the same!

It didn't take long for me to realize that my lifelong battle with food was rearing its ugly head once again—and my weight was starting to shoot back up . . . FAST!

I knew I somehow HAD to get a handle on things . . . but *how?!*

I found myself remembering the producers' parting words to me as I left for home . . . *"Be sure to find a good counselor,"* they'd said.

Pssh! I'd been quick to dismiss *that* advice!

Counseling is for weirdos or people who are weak—or dealing with some major life tragedy, I'd thought. *I didn't need counseling!*

So I had a little problem with food; I could handle that on my own!

Or so I *thought* . . .

Eventually, however, as my weight continued to climb, I decided maybe I'd give the counseling thing a shot after all.

Initially, it did not go well!

In fact, I tried three different counselors . . . and "broke up" with all of them! "It's not *me;* it's *YOU*," I insisted.

Truthfully, none of the three were a particularly good "fit" for me. I'm a bit of a head case (but, if you haven't picked up on that from the previous 34 chapters, then I might suggest that *I'm* not the only one)!

Unfortunately, I was locked in a losing battle against binge eating—so my weight continued to climb.

Finally, in a last-ditch effort, I agreed to see a woman (on the board of a local counseling center) who'd been suggested to me.

Of course, by the time my appointment arrived, I was in typical Sonya Jones form—ostensibly ready to attack this issue . . . but with all my defenses up!

As with all of my previous counselors, I went bounding into that appointment wearing my usual light-hearted façade, determined to make the counselor laugh!

But no sooner was I on the couch with Julie when I realized (for the first time in my life) that I am, at heart, an actress and entertainer! Oh, sure—I'd been on TV; but until now, I'd thought that I was just being myself. All of a sudden, it dawned on me that I'd always been playing a part, desperate to keep anyone from realizing that all was not okay inside!

I mean, I certainly had no intention of letting anyone know that I had a real problem (as if my seeking out a *fourth* counselor didn't make that clear already)!

But, in that moment, I sensed something changing inside me—as the Lord seemed to quiet my heart and say: "Enough."

It was time to deal with this once and for all!

I knew that, if there was any hope of my finally getting well and being free, then I had to stop covering up the hurt. So I immediately determined one thing: I was going to be completely honest and transparent with *this* counselor, no matter how vulnerable I felt.

This was it— no holding back, no more walls or acting or showmanship . . .

"I'm going to give this everything I've got," I said to myself.

I had no idea how hard this was going to be.

One of the first things that Julie helped me recognize is that I am primarily a *"doer"* not a *"feeler."*

Oh, I feel things deeply—but struggle to *communicate* how I feel.

As we began to talk through situations, she would repeatedly ask: "Sonya, how did that make you *feel?*" And, every time, I would respond with what I had *done* . . . not how I had *felt!*

I tried on a large top and it was too tight.

"How did that make you FEEL?"

Well, I've put on so much weight that I can hardly fit into a large top so I freaked out!"

"Okay—so 'freaked out' is what you *DID;* now tell me how you *FELT!*"

Well, I went for a bigger size—but I still FELT fat because a large wouldn't fit.

"Once again, you've told me what you *DID*—but how did you *FEEL?*"

I wanted to scream! Was she not *listening* to me? What was I *paying* her for?!

Ok fine, I felt FAT! There, I said it.

But she patiently persisted, explaining that "FAT is not a *feeling*" as she drilled down to help me identify my actual emotion of the moment.

Wow, she's good! Five minutes in and she's already forcing me to go further than I ever did with any of the other counselors.

Julie seemed to have all the right resources. For instance, I was so bad at identifying my feelings that she resorted to using a "feelings chart" that forced me to point out the words that best described how I was feeling.

"How did you feel, Sonya?"

*Anxious. Scared. Sad. **Ashamed.***

Ouch. That hurt!

Did I really just say that?!

Did I, Sonya Jones, just verbalize that I felt sad . . . and *ashamed?!*

Tough stuff.

But we began to peel back the layers of what was driving me to eat beyond my control . . . until, with her help, I could finally face the fact that my real problem was not with *food* at all . . . but with *ME!*

Julie would tell me later that she recognized my real issue in our very first session, within minutes of our meeting—but she wisely gave me the time and prodding I needed to make that discovery for myself. And *that* made all the difference!

So maybe ***counseling isn't just for weirdos***, after all!

Then again, maybe it is . . .

Because the truth is that we all have some weirdness in us . . . and that's *okay!*

I know you're probably thinking that, weird or not, counseling is not for everyone—or that not everyone has access to a truly wonderful counselor like the one I finally found.

But that's not entirely true.

A full 700 years before the birth of Christ, the prophet Isaiah foretold the coming of One Who would be called "Wonderful Counselor" (Isaiah 9:6); and, once He arrived on the scene, Jesus of Nazareth proved to be just that (and more)!

John 2:25 says that "He did not [even] need any testimony . . . for He knew what was in each person" already! After all, Colossians 2:3 points out that "all the treasures of wisdom and knowledge are hidden in Him" (HCSB).

And even though Jesus Himself no longer walks the earth, before He returned to Heaven, He promised that God would "give you another Counselor to be with you forever . . . Who will teach you all things and remind you of everything I have told you" (John 14:16, 26—CSB).

With the gift of His Holy Spirit, God has provided you with One Who is preeminently qualified to address and meet the deepest needs of your heart in ways that not even the best human counselor can match. He knows exactly what's going on with you (and the root issues beneath it) before you even start to open up and share. What's more, you have 24/7 access to Him; you don't need an appointment—or even have to leave the house! (How cool is that?!)

You can trust Him to listen to your problems and to guide you in the best possible direction, confident that He loves you and always has your best interests at heart!

You may benefit from having a visible, physically – present person to sit across from and chat with (I certainly needed that). The good news is that He's equipped some wonderful human counselors to work in tandem with Him to bring you to a place of real healing and wholeness—and I encourage you to seek them out.

But the best news of all is that you can start that process right now: by turning to the Counselor He's already provided—and letting Him take it from here . . .

You see, *counseling isn't just for weirdos.* It's for ALL of us—and He's made the very BEST counselor personally available to YOU!

LESSON #36

FIND YOUR "A-HA" MOMENT!

It seemed like a typical late Wednesday afternoon when I walked in for my weekly counseling appointment with Julie. I'd had a pretty good week, so I didn't feel like I really had a whole lot to share that day.

In re-capping the week, I said that nothing really stood out . . . except perhaps one *minor* event that I felt I had handled quite well.

She asked me to tell her about it, so I did . . .

"A friend of mine was getting married this weekend, so I made plans to meet some of my girlfriends there so we could attend the wedding and reception together. Only, when I arrived, I realized that they'd all brought their *husbands* also—so I was the only *single* person at our table! It was a beautiful ceremony, and we all had a great time and enjoyed a lot of laughs—but I decided to make it an early night. After calling up my roommate to see what she wanted for dinner, I grabbed us a couple of sandwiches on the way home."

"All right," Julie said. "Do you mind if we unpack that just a little bit?"

Sure . . .

"Okay," she said, "so you're at this wedding when you realize that you're the only *single* person there. How did that make you *FEEL?*"

Ugh. Here we go with the FEELINGS again. She's just begging for a good throat punch!

"Well, we had a blast," I said. "We *laughed* a lot!"

She was not about to let me off the hook that easily.

"But I'm not asking how you *responded,*" she probed. "I'm asking how you *felt*. What emotions were you *feeling* during this time?"

"Well, I was the 'life of the party,' like always!" I said. "I walked around talking with people and had a great time hanging out with my friends!"

"Sonya," she said, "that's what you *did*. How did you *feel?*"

Right now, I feel like punching you in the throat! Wanna hand me that trusty "feelings chart" I love so much?

The truth of the matter is . . . I knew exactly how I felt; I just didn't want to *verbalize* it. But I did.

I FELT *lonely* and *embarrassed* and *sad*.

I felt *angry*—for putting myself in that position, simply because I hadn't asked enough questions beforehand to get a clearer picture.

I felt *shame* . . . as if, once again, I was the only single person in the world! *Story of my life!*

She seemed pleased once I said all that.

"Okay," she said. "Now we're on to something . . . you said you left the reception early, called your roomie, and you guys came up with a plan for dinner. Is that correct?"

Yes.

"So—when you left the wedding, where did you go?"

Does she not listen at all? I stopped at a sandwich shop on the way home.

By this point in our relationship, Julie knew me (and my patterns) well enough to know that she needed to probe a bit further . . .

"But did you stop anywhere before you got to the sandwich shop?"

No! Umm, wait a minute—yes, I did. Come to think of it, I stopped at the gas station.

"Okay," she said. "What did you purchase at the gas station?"

I purchased four donuts, two king-size candy bars, and a 44-ounce regular soda.

"So you got back in your car with the food and went where?"

I went to the sandwich shop.

"So what did you do with the food and drink that you purchased at the gas station?"

I ate it. All.

"And, when you got to the sandwich shop, what did you do with the wrappers?"

I threw them all away.

"So, when you walked up to the counter, what did you order?"

I ordered two sandwiches, two bags of chips, and four brownies.

"Four brownies?"

Yes.

"Did all four brownies make it to your house?"

No. I ate two of them in the parking lot before I left the sandwich shop.

"Okay—so you left the sandwich shop and you have, at this point, eaten four donuts, two king-sized candy bars, two brownies and a 44-ounce soda. Did you stop anywhere else before you got home?"

Yes. Yes, I did. Another sandwich shop that has really good cookies.

"What did you purchase at *that* sandwich shop?"

I purchased three of their large chocolate chip cookies. I got in my car and I ate them on my way home.

"Did you stop anywhere else before you got home?"

Yes, I did. I stopped at another gas station—but only to throw away all of the additional food wrappers from the cookies that I had just consumed.

"So—when you walked into your home, you walked through the door with two sandwiches, two bags of chips, and two brownies—and you ate a normal dinner with your roommate just like everything was 'business as usual!' But that little 20-minute binge episode cost you more than 5,000 calories . . . just because you were experiencing some negative emotion. Honey, your problem is not with *food;* it's with managing your *emotions.* Do you see that? "

All of a sudden, in that moment, I *did.*

She was right. My real issue was not with food at all; it was with managing my emotions.

I felt lonely, embarrassed, sad, angry, and ashamed—but, rather than *dealing* with those emotions, I *ate* them instead!

That had been my pattern my entire life! I put on this façade that everything was okay . . . when I was really hurting inside!

In that moment, the light bulb went on!

A-ha!

I suddenly realized that food had always been the "drug" I turned to when I needed to feel better. It never talked back or judged me. It was just there; it was *always* there!

But right then, I realized that the only way for me to win this battle and truly get healthy was to learn to *manage* my emotions instead of *stuffing* them!

Thanks to a very skilled counselor (aided by the Great Counselor), that moment changed the course of my life.

Shortly thereafter, Julie and I developed a plan to help me learn to manage my emotions effectively—and, by the grace of God, I haven't binged again (even once) since that moment in her office.

That was *my* "A-ha" moment!

You have to *find your* own *"A-ha" moment* to know what is driving your decisions.

Figure out what's driving you to negative behavior—and then make the necessary changes that will enable YOU to navigate life successfully!

LESSON #37

DEVELOP A GAME PLAN.

Though finding your "A-ha" moment is a tremendous step forward (in terms of self-awareness, at least), in order to achieve lasting success, you have to develop an actual *game plan!*

As a coach, I've spent much of my life developing game plans to help others succeed—but I had to learn to do the same for myself!

Life is hard! There will always be times when situations arise that are completely beyond your control, and a lot of emotions will accompany that.

In my case, I had to develop a game plan to *attack* those emotions head-on, instead of simply *stuffing* them with food!

I needed to create healthy options to my lifelong habit of unhealthy binging!

What proved most helpful to me was identifying (and putting in place) those things that really "make me tick" and bring me joy, thus helping me to remove myself from a stressful situation in a healthy and enjoyable way!

For instance, when I'm feeling overly emotional or stressed and am tempted to binge, I now turn to one (or more) of these alternatives:

- *Listen to worship music*

- *Go for a walk, run, or drive*

- *Pray*

- *Call a friend to talk through things*

- *Read my Bible*

- *Watch videos of people falling down or getting scared* (because nothing makes me laugh any harder than that!)

It wasn't long after my "A-ha" moment in the counselor's office that I had my first opportunity to test my game plan . . .

My best friend (and roommate) and I had taken my parents to dinner. You need to know that my brave and beautiful mother is in a tough battle of her own with dementia. She's safe and happy right now (which is what matters most), but her condition can easily make me *want* to binge.

On this particular evening, at one of her favorite restaurants, my mom indulged her still-healthy appetite on their famous fried catfish, thoroughly enjoying every single bite.

With my precious momma

We were on our way home when she told me that she needed to use the restroom . . .

Unfortunately, by the time I could get her to the nearest stop, it was too late! She'd had an accident, but I managed to clean her up enough to get her the rest of the way home.

As soon as we reached the house, I put her in the shower and got her properly cleaned up. (Not the easiest thing in the world, but she'd done the same for me a thousand times before I was able to care for myself—so this seemed like the least I could do!)

By the time I got her out of the shower, she was happy as a clam—and ready to eat again! Happily for her, she didn't even really remember what had taken place. Unfortunately, *I* did . . . and I was exhausted (both physically and emotionally) and ready to head for home!

Ordinarily, under the stress of these circumstances, I would easily have binged on anywhere from 5,000-8,000 calories (I *wish* that were an exaggeration) on the way home!

I knew it was time to put the game plan in place—so, on the way home, I put on some worship music. That seemed to help, but I could tell I was struggling with a lot of powerfully negative emotions, so I started to pray.

At this point, I turned to Jeni (my best friend and roomie) to enlist her help in the battle. I expressed my feelings to her, confessing how strongly I was battling the desire to binge.

"If you don't follow me all the way home," I said, "I'm afraid I will stop at nearly every fast food restaurant and gas station on the way there!"

She faithfully followed me the entire way—so I did not stop, but pulled into the garage without having consumed even a single calorie . . . all because I stuck to the game plan!

Developing (and sticking to) a game plan was key to my success—and will be to YOURS too!

Life is hard—and there will be times when you will want more than anything to just break down and cry—or, better yet, punch someone in the throat! But a good game plan will enable you to stand strong when the wind and waves come rolling in!

It's become a cliché (but only because it's true): if you fail to plan, you plan to fail!

Develop (and adhere to) *a* good *game plan* and you will be able to navigate even the choppiest waters with stunningly smooth success!

LESSON #38

WELLNESS IS MORE THAN WEIGHT LOSS.

Everywhere I go, I get the same question . . .

*What's your secret—**how do you keep the weight off?***

To be honest, it's a constant battle! *Losing* the weight was EASY compared to *keeping* it off!

I can, however, share a few practical tips that might help . . .

First of all, a *diet* won't do it. You've got to commit to a *lifestyle change!*

I know! It sounds cliché, but it's true!

Trust me—by the time I went on *The Biggest Loser*, I had tried every diet known to man (including some that haven't even been invented yet)!

Jenny Craig, Weight Watchers, Nutrisystem; low-calorie, low-carbohydrate, low-fat; you name it. I even tried that nasty cabbage soup diet—but didn't even make it to banana day before I found myself in a Dairy Queen drive-thru! (I tried Atkins and South Beach too; but I'm not that bright, got the fats confused, and ended up with some weird hybrid of South Atkins that never quite worked.)

In each and every one of those endless diets, I managed to lose weight . . . only to gain it all back again! I once lost 71 pounds (on a liquid diet)—but gained *80* back!

So trust me—I've been there . . . and it was brutal!

You ultimately have to commit to changing your *lifestyle!*

You have to commit to make whatever changes you have to in order to get and stay healthy! Anything less than that, and you will put back on every single pound and then some!

This cannot be a short-term commitment. It has to be a plan that you can live with *long-term.*

I track my food daily. I jog three or four times a week. I make careful and healthy decisions when I dine out. Those are all things that help me live a lifestyle of health and wellness.

People are forever asking me for the "magic pill"—but, for me, it's simple . . .

Are you ready for this?

I'm going to give you three little words that can change your life . . .

Ready? (The suspense is building . . . I can feel it!)

The "magic pill" to losing weight (and keeping it off) is . . .

Diet and Exercise!

Ta-da!

Go ahead . . . roll your eyes!

It's true.

I have learned (the hard way) that you simply have to *take in LESS* and *move MORE!*

So find something that you can do for a *lifetime!*

'Cuz there IS no magic shake, pill, or potion—only finding what will work for you that you can stick to for the rest of your life!

But I would be remiss if I didn't share with you one of the most important pieces of the puzzle on your personal path to health and wellness . . .

Please know that there is a lot more to wellness than weight loss!

You see, wellness is ultimately not about losing weight.

It's about being healthy in body, mind, and spirit!

Focus on losing the weight—while foregoing your mind and spirit—and you will put the weight back on! Every last pound of it.

But here's another life-changing truth that I pray you will grasp: *your worth and value is not determined by the number on a scale!*

Let me say that again: **your worth and value is not determined by the number on a scale!**

You are not a *better* person when you *lose* 44 pounds.

You are not a *worse* person when you *gain* 44 pounds.

Now, I'm not going to tell you that it won't change how you *feel* about yourself—but your real worth and value has nothing to do with the number on a scale!

You are worth more than that number on the scale!

Your real worth and value is found in who *GOD* says you are!

He says that:

> *You are His child* (Galatians 3:26).

> *You are a personal friend of His* (John 15:15).

> *You are fearfully and wonderfully made* (Psalm 139:13-14).

> *You are totally and completely forgiven* (I John 1:9).

You are created in His likeness (Ephesians 4:24).

You are greatly loved (Romans 5:8).

You are set free in Christ (Galatians 5:1).

You are more than a conqueror (Romans 8:37).

You are a new creation in Christ (II Corinthians 5:17).

Wellness is so much ***more than weight loss***—because your worth and value is found entirely in who GOD says you are . . . *not* the number you see on the scale!

You are a dearly-loved child of God—whom He has bought for an unspeakably high price! *Act like it!*

LESSON #39

JUST BECAUSE IT'S DIFFICULT DOESN'T MEAN IT ISN'T WORTH IT.

You've heard it said before: life is not a *sprint;* it's a *marathon!*

Your path to overall health and wellness will be, like mine has been, a lifelong *journey!*

But *my* journey is no more important than *yours!*

Mine may be a bit more memorable—if only by virtue of having been played out on national television in Spandex and a sports bra—but yours is every bit as important!

Your journey, like mine, is likely to be long and difficult—but that doesn't mean it isn't worth it. In fact, it may very well be the most meaningful journey of your entire life!

Let's say that one of your goals is to lose weight.

Well, you didn't put 50 pounds on overnight, and you're not likely to take it off overnight either! But you do yourself a HUGE disservice if you look at the end result as your final destination!

After all, the journey is about a lot more than weight loss or finding a spouse or potty training your kids or getting them out of their teenage years alive—or whatever your goal may be for this particular season.

Crazy and busy and hard as life can sometimes be, there is JOY in the *journey!* Lessons to be learned, relationships to be built, blessings every step of the way . . .

It's also important to recognize that the journey is NOT just physical. As I've tried to illustrate from my own experience, it's at least as much a mental, emotional, and spiritual pilgrimage!

The biggest part of my journey to health on *The Biggest Loser* was not *physical.*

After all, you don't get to be 283 pounds on a 5'4" frame because you like to eat a few pieces of pizza!

You only get to that point as the result of a very serious emotional tie to food! (Can we say "addiction"?)

You have to be willing to peel back the layers and address the emotional and mental things that are tying you down.

Most journeys that are truly *worth* it are, at times, quite difficult!

But I've learned that *difficult* doesn't always mean *negative*.

Don't let *pain* stand in the way of *possibility!*

In my favorite movie of all time, *A League of Their Own,* Dottie (the BEST baseball player in the league) decides to quit just before the World Series. Her husband, injured in the war, is returning home sooner than anticipated—so she decides to leave her team behind to start a family. (As an athlete, I can't even fathom that!)

But Dottie is loading her car to leave when her manager warns her that she'll regret quitting the team for the rest of her life, but she protests that "It just got too hard."

I'll never forget his reply.

"Of course it's hard," he says. "It's *supposed* to be hard. If it was *easy,* everyone would do it! The *hard* is what makes it *great!*"

That *still* gives me goose bumps!

***The* hard *is what makes it* great!**

Do you have any idea how hard this journey was for ME?

It was the hardest thing I have ever done in my life—but it was the most *rewarding* thing as well!

Don't give up when things get hard!

Sure, it would be a lot easier to give in—but *just because it's* **difficult** *doesn't mean it isn't* **worth** *it!*

The *hardest* journey just may turn out to be the most *meaningful* and *rewarding* of all.

LESSON #40

THERE IS STRENGTH IN BEING BROKEN.

I was 10 years old—sitting in my living room for hours on end, utterly mesmerized as I watched the 1984 Summer Olympic Games, marveling at the world's greatest gymnasts on the uneven bars.

In that moment—I knew, beyond any shadow of a doubt, that the Lord was calling me to be an Olympic gymnast (albeit a slightly *chunky* variety)!

Since I was only 10, I figured I'd better start practicing immediately—if I was to overcome Mary Lou Retton's *slight* advantage over me . . .

Move over, Mary Lou Retton

Running out the back door, I grabbed my bicycle and rode out to the big oak tree to begin training. I *knew* I had it in me!

Laying my bike on the ground, I began my climb up this massive oak. Only about halfway up, I saw it: *my* branch! *My* spot! The place where I would begin my trek to Olympic glory!

Climbing up to my beloved branch, I shimmied out to where I would have some room to do my "routine"! (Bear in mind, I had absolutely no idea what my routine was—but I was sure it would be a *winner!)*

All I knew was that I was supposed to get up enough speed to go around and around on that branch just like I had seen Mary Lou do on TV!

So here I am, hanging on to this branch for dear life as I swing my legs forward, then backwards, then forward again . . . to begin my dismount.

It was actually more of a *fall* than a *dismount*, but I think I mustered up enough speed to maybe make it around once. I'm afraid, however, that I can't say that with complete integrity—because what happened afterward is a little foggy . . . As best I can figure, I landed on the ground (because that's how gravity works) on my right side.

It knocked the wind out of me . . . but I thought I was okay.

I stood up and dusted myself off, hoping that no one had seen what had just happened.

But, as I was dusting myself off, I just happened to look down and noticed a bunch of puffy, white meat coming out of my right thigh!

I might not have been the brightest kid on the block, but I was smart enough to realize that something was amiss—particularly when I spotted a huge hole in the side of my leg (that I was fairly certain had not been there a moment ago)! Clearly, *something* had gone awry!

I took my fat little fingers and tried to shove the meat back inside the gaping hole in my leg—but it just wouldn't stay in!

You see, when I fell, I had landed directly on my rusty old bicycle kickstand and sliced my leg open!

But, with only about 15 minutes of daylight left, and determined to get the most out of this day, I decided to head back up the tree to make yet another attempt. (Hey, I told you I wasn't the brightest kid on the block!)

Once my 15 minutes was up and the dark had forced me inside, I had a conversation with my mom that went something like this . . .

Sonya: "So, Mom—if I show you something, will you promise not to take me to the hospital?"

Mom: "Sure . . ."

Of course, 30 seconds later, we were in the truck headed to the hospital—with me (crying for the first time since this whole episode began) accusing my mother of having LIED to me!

I spent the night in the hospital—with doctors giving me numbing shots in the wound before cleaning it and putting in 37 stitches, while diagnosing me with a hairline fracture in the bone!

I remember lying there thinking (in my most dramatic 10-year-old fashion) that my *life* was over!

I mean—there goes my Olympic career, my whole future as a leg-model . . . *I'll probably have to be on crutches for the rest of my life!* (I told you I was dramatic.)

Of course, the wound healed nicely (though it left one heck of a scar on my leg).

But X-rays done in subsequent years to evaluate the bone revealed that the spot where the bone had been broken had calcified and was actually *stronger* than it was before the break! The healing process had taken what had once been wounded and made it even stronger than it was before!

Look at your own wounds.

Somebody hurt you, cheated on you, lied about you, caused you a great deal of pain . . .

At the time, you wonder how you'll ever get *through* it—and are certain that you'll never get *over* it!

But God can use those wounds to make you even *stronger* than you were before!

See, God doesn't waste a hurt!

The lessons you learn and the character that God builds in you through the pain in those seasons of hurt can sometimes be accomplished no *other* way.

There is purpose in your pain.

There is hope in your healing.

***There is strength in being* broken.**

LESSON #41

KNOW YOUR "WHY"!

So . . . what do you DO?

I'll bet people ask you that question all the time, right?

It's usually one of the first questions you get when sitting down next to a stranger on an airplane (assuming everyone hasn't already put in their earbuds and tuned out the rest of the world around them).

But I have a *different* interest . . .

Tell me *WHY!*

Why do you do what you do?

I never really understood the concept of knowing my "why" (or even realized that I *had* a "why") until after my time on *The Biggest Loser*. But at some point in that whole process, it dawned on me that it all comes down to whatever most breaks your heart.

If you can identify what truly breaks your heart, then you're on the road to identifying your own personal "why."

For instance, in my case, there are two things that I see (or hear about) that break my heart on an almost daily basis.

The *first* is abuse.

I don't like abuse of ANY kind—but abuse of children, the elderly, and animals REALLY gets to me! If I watch those television ads for starving children or neglected animals for more than about two seconds (without changing the channel), then I'm usually reduced to a blubbering mess!

Abuse just tears me up.

The *second* is people who refuse to believe that they can make a change.

Practically every day, people come up to me wanting to know the secret to losing weight and keeping it off. They feel trapped in their own bodies, having tried everything they can think of to lose weight—all without success.

That tears me up—because, believe me, I know what it's like to be morbidly obese.

KNOW YOUR "WHY"!   257

- I know what it feels like to be asked to get off a theme park ride because the seat belt won't go around you.

- I know what it's like to walk into a restaurant and have to request a *table* because you can't fit into a *booth*.

- I know . . . because I've been there . . . and I *remember*.

That's tough stuff—and it breaks my heart when people feel trapped in a vicious cycle with absolutely no way out!

But those heartbreaks have led me to a couple of very specific "whys" . . .

Because of the heartbreak I feel over abuse, I have resolved that—every single day—I will do something to help *combat* that abuse! For instance, one of my most recent passions is that of rescuing pit bulls. I give money; I volunteer at shelters; in short, I'm doing whatever I can to make a difference in the lives of those abused animals.

And simply remembering the heartbreak of feeling trapped in an oversized body with no way out drives me to do whatever it takes for me to remain free of that prison!

Thus, my "why" helps me stay focused.

My "why" helps me to maintain my weight loss (by choosing salmon and broccoli when I'd much *rather* have fried chicken with mashed potatoes and gravy)!

My "why" gets me out of bed at 5:44 in the morning for a *jog* when I'd much *rather* pull the covers over my head and *sleep* for another 44 minutes!

My "why" helps me recognize, every single day, that I really CAN do this thing called life and even use my own (occasionally bumpy) journey to inspire others on theirs!

So—how about YOU? What drives or motivates you? In other words, what's *your* "why"?

Maybe your "why" is to get into the perfect outfit . . . or to see your children grow up . . .

I urge you—if you haven't already done so—find (and identify) your *"why"!*

It will help fuel your fire when it's hard to keep going! Your "why" will remind you that your personal conviction is greater than your present circumstance!

Know your "WHY" . . . and, once you find it, don't ever let it go!

LESSON #42

DON'T BELIEVE EVERYTHING YOU READ.

I realize that it seems a bit self-destructive for an author to tell her readers not to believe everything they read (you'll notice I waited 'til you were nearly done with the book before dropping *that* on you)—but it's true!

Fortunately, in this day and age—when scarcely a day goes by that we don't hear something about "fake news"—most of us have learned to be a bit more discerning when it comes to the things we read.

That's a good thing . . . because I've lost count of all the things I've read—only to discover later that they were, at best, filled with all sorts of distortions, omissions, and half-truths (if not outright lies), selectively chosen to advance a false narrative!

I am, by nature, a pretty positive person (a quick visit to my Facebook or Instagram pages will confirm that

I never post anything negative about anyone)—so it's really not my style to call anyone out—nor is that my intention here.

On the other hand, I'm also pretty passionate about sharing the story of my experience with *The Biggest Loser*—and I know that a lot of what I've shared here is at odds with some other accounts you may have read.

Since my time on *The Biggest Loser*, the show has received quite a bit of negative press—even coming under withering criticism from some former contestants who have suggested that they were asked to use drugs during their time on the program.

Obviously, there would be legitimate concerns if even half the charges lodged against the show should prove true (perhaps one reason it seems to be on hiatus at the time of this writing).

While it is neither my purpose nor place to call anyone else a liar, I can assure you—based on my own personal experience (which is ultimately all I can speak to)—that I never witnessed nor experienced any of the negative things that have been described.

During my season on the show, we were seldom allowed to take any sort of medication at all! (The medical team wouldn't even allow me a little NyQuil to help me get to sleep at night.) We could hardly even coax them into giving us *pain relievers* for our aching muscles. (Their preferred solution was to prescribe ice baths—which, trust me, hurt a lot more than a little muscle soreness!)

The only people that I know of who ever received any drugs of any kind were those who were either diabetic or had previous conditions that required medication. (The irony is that they were off most of them within the very first month—since the body has a remarkable ability to heal itself when properly cared for!)

You may have read complaints from some former contestants of mistreatment during their time on the show. Again, I can speak only from my own experience, but I can tell you right now that, if given the opportunity, I would drop whatever I'm doing and go on the show again *tomorrow!* It felt more like being part of a family than a contestant on a TV show, and I truly loved every minute of it!

Without exception, everyone (from the producers and casting agents to the technical staff, trainers, and fellow contestants) made me feel loved, honored, respected, and cared for every single day of my time on the Ranch. They laughed and cried right along with me through every joy and sorrow, victory and defeat!

I'm not suggesting that every moment of every day was a walk in the park. Tensions sometimes ran high; nerves were on edge; and we all had our moments (as everyone does).

But I firmly believe (*now*, just as I did *then*) that everyone I came in contact with during that whole process really believed in *me* and was united in a common goal: to make not just a better TV show, but a better ME! As such, every day I spent with them was a treasure!

In 2016, the *New York Post* released a study purporting to show that the program wrecked contestants' metabolism and doomed them to eventually re-gain all of their weight (and then some).

I'm no metabolic expert—so I can't really speak to *that* part of it.

What I *can* tell you, however, is that since being on the show, I have found that, as long as I eat what I'm supposed to eat, I keep my body weight where it needs to be.

From my perspective, it seems to have little to do with metabolism OR exercise. It's really pretty simple: if I consume appropriate amounts of healthy, nutritious foods that fuel my body, then my weight stays where it should!

The real magic happens in the *kitchen* (you can't out-train a bad diet)!

Is my metabolism messed up? I don't know . . . maybe?

What I *do* know is this: before the show, I suffered from high cholesterol, high blood pressure, severe sleep apnea, fatty liver disease, arthritis, joint pain, diverticulosis, and was pre-diabetic! I suffer from NONE of those things today—not ONE!

So I *may* have a messed-up metabolism.

Even IF that's true, that seems like a pretty good trade-off to me—in exchange for the long laundry list of conditions that I had *before* the show! So, sign me up—I'll take it!

I often hear the claim that everyone who goes on *The Biggest Loser* eventually puts all their weight back on anyway. I am but one of many who can attest to the contrary . . . by demonstrating otherwise!

Have I gained *some* weight back since the show? Yes—but I *needed* to!

My Finale weight was 139 pounds—which was about 30 pounds under the goal weight that the show's doctor prescribed for me—warning that, if I were to go under that weight, I would feel terrible. He was right!

Once I dropped below 160 or so, I started to feel miserable. I continued to drop weight—only because I was determined to go just as low as I possibly could, doing everything in my power to claim that $250,000 Grand Prize! It was never my intention (or desire) to stay *that* low.

I *had* to put on some pounds afterward—just to get back up to a *healthy* weight!

No, I'll never again look like I did at our season finale—nor do I *want* to! If I can stay at a healthy weight of 170-180 pounds, I'll be perfectly happy with that.

Do some former contestants put all of their weight back on (and gain even more)? Sure, *some* do (though I'd be willing to bet it's because they still haven't managed to get to the root of their weight problem in the first place).

Regardless of the reason, my heart goes out to those brothers and sisters—as I know first-hand what a difficult journey this can be. But they lost it once, and I know that they can lose it again! You have to be a strong person to make it on *The Biggest Loser* at all, so it's my hope and prayer that they will be able to tap into that strength yet again, and attain health and happiness for the long haul!

All I can say is that my time on *The Biggest Loser* was the greatest journey of my life. I will be forever grateful for the impact it made on me and on millions of other Americans who were inspired by it.

*With one of the greatest groups of people I know
on the greatest show I know*

While there are two sides to every story, I can speak only to mine—which is still being written, but has been pretty sensational so far . . .

In the meantime—unless you read it here ('cuz I can vouch for the truth in these pages)—*don't believe everything you read!*

LESSON #43

PAY IT FORWARD.

More than 88,000 people applied for the 20 spots available on the 16th season of *The Biggest Loser*—which means that, from a purely mathematical perspective, I had only a .0002% chance of making it onto the Ranch at all!

So, the way I see it—since God gave me such a rare and unique opportunity—He must have done it for a *reason*.

I believe part of that reason was so that I could "pay it forward" by passing along some of what I learned along the way, and encouraging you to do the same.

Obesity is a major epidemic in our country today, which is why millions of people (like me) have grown desperate enough to want to change their situation that they're willing to compete for the embarrassing privilege of appearing on national television in Spandex and a sports bra if that's what it takes to get them started on the road to change!

Grateful as I am to have had the privilege of traveling it, it was a TOUGH road (more guts than glamour most days). That's why I'm hoping that some of the lessons I learned on my journey will enable YOU to get there by a little *easier* route!

On the Ranch, we worked out an average of 6-8 hours a day—getting in as many as 69,000 steps and burning as many as 8,000 calories—all in a single day! (Of course, no one can sustain that in their everyday life in the real world; but, while we were there, that was our full-time job.)

Not everyone can do that, and not everyone would *want* to . . . even if they *could.*

The Biggest Loser Ranch is not for everyone.

But *some* things are . . .

A sense of pride and accomplishment? *That* IS for everyone!

The thrill of knowing that you've been able to set a goal, go hard after it, totally crushing it just in time to set a new one? *That* IS for everyone!

That—even more than weight loss—is what being a contestant on *The Biggest Loser* gave me.

And that's what I want to give to YOU—paying forward the lessons I've learned . . .

The Biggest Loser changed my life—all for the GOOD! And, while I know you will probably never have a chance to spend even one day on the Ranch, I want you to end up at the same good place in life, however different the route by which you get there!

I want you to know (and believe) that you can make any change in your life that you need to . . . on the way to becoming a happier and healthier you! (Speaking from experience, you will be so glad that you made those changes!)

I want to pay forward to you the confidence that, with God's help, you really DO have within you all that it takes to succeed. You, too, can be a mountain-mover . . . and begin living your best life TODAY!

I really want to be a game-changer in your life—but I don't want it to end there! I want YOU, in turn, to become a game-changer in the lives of *others*.

So, how about it? Will you partner with me in doing whatever you can to make the lives of those on your path the best they can possibly be?

Together, we can *pay it forward!*

LESSON #44

YOU ARE HERE FOR "SUCH A TIME AS THIS"!

One of my favorite characters in the Bible is a woman named *Esther.*

Even after being elevated to the lofty position of *queen* (of the mighty Persian Empire), she was reluctant to think that she could make any real difference in the lives of others . . . until her cousin Mordecai helped her to see that she had been providentially positioned for precisely "such a time as this!"

In *her* case, thousands of lives and the survival of an entire race were at stake!

You may not have nearly as much riding on you, but Mordecai's searching question for her—"*Who knows if perhaps you were made for such a time as this?*" (Esther 4:14)—is still every bit as relevant for YOU today!

God has given each of us a unique opportunity to impact the lives of those around us—which means that you, too, have been made *"for such a time as this!"*

You don't have to be on a reality TV show to have an impact. You don't even need to be *wealthy* or *well-known*.

You just need to see and seize the opportunity when it comes your way!

You were made by a God Who is crazy about you and put you here both to know and enjoy Him *yourself* . . . AND to share Him with *others!*

He has placed you exactly where you are . . . to have a positive influence and impact on those He's put around you.

You are here *for such a time as this!*

After all, you're still making trips around the sun and sucking in air, aren't you? That means that God is not finished with you yet!

I don't care if you're 14, 44, or 104—if you're still vertical and breathing, then God still has a plan and purpose for your life!

When I first sat down to write this book, before I ever put down the first word, I prayed specifically for YOU! I asked God to reveal Himself to you in a fresh and exciting way through this book—and to use our time together to make you a person of *impact.*

I really appreciate your spending this time with me. I hope that you've laughed a little (and maybe *cried* a little too). But I truly pray you have been encouraged a LOT—and are stepping away with newfound hope.

And since I prayed for you before *starting* this book, I'd like to *end* it the same way . . .

Father,

I ask You to bless and encourage my friend finishing this book right now. Would You just reveal Yourself in a new way—as You remind us just how crazy You are about us? And help us to be people of real impact—acting as Your hands and heart . . . in a world that desperately needs to feel Your touch and know Your love!

In the mighty and matchless Name of Jesus I ask it,

Amen.

You are loved . . . more deeply than you will ever know.

Now go change the world—because **you are here . . . for such a time as this!**

*A coach and her trainer . . . getting "slimed" in a special
assembly at Sherman Elementary School*

*An unforgettable moment with Jen . . . right before
watching my Journey video*

And then there were three . . .

Blessed with the best support group in the world

Catching up with co-author Christopher Burcham and his wife Amanda while home training for Finale . . .

Down to the Final Four

Contestants had their own refrigerator in the Elimination Room. I'm so glad my light never went off!

Forever grateful for the life-altering impact of Jessie's thoughtful and well-timed words

Jen with her two finalists

Jen's visit to my hometown

The Jones-A-Palooza Girls

The current love of my life . . . a handsome fella named Rocky

With more of the "home tribe" at Finale

With my hometown girls who came to support me at Finale

*With my phenomenal former counselor, Julie Tucker-Ponder,
who helped me get at the root of my issues*

With The Biggest Loser's *nutritionist and dietician,*
Cheryl Forberg

With Bob Harper

EPILOGUE

I've talked a lot in this book about the Lord—for one simple reason . . .

I believe that God has a plan and purpose for our lives. He's given us a reason for living and a relationship (with Jesus) to live for!

You may not be a "church" person. Maybe religion really isn't your thing.

Maybe the only reason you even picked up this book is because someone gave it to you (or you just happen to be a really big fan of reality TV)—but now this journey is taking you WAAYY out of your "comfort zone."

That's okay. No judgment here, I promise.

But—since you've come with me this far, I have to tell you that, whether you believe it or not, it's no accident that you're reading this book. God has a message for YOU—which is that He loves you and, regardless of your experience up to this point, He really DOES have a plan for your life . . . and it's a better plan than you even dare *dream* right now!

Believe me when I tell you that choosing to build a relationship with Jesus is, by far, the single most important decision you will ever make! It's more important than who you marry, the career you pursue, or where you choose to live . . . because this decision doesn't just affect your *today* . . . it affects your *forever!*

See, the truth of the matter is that you can try to "fix up" your life; but unless you let Jesus "take the wheel," you're never gonna get there! Your journey will never be complete!

Money can't complete you. Fame can't complete you. Being on a reality TV show certainly can't complete you . . . even if you happen to WIN! There will still be something missing.

True satisfaction and fulfillment comes only with a personal relationship with Jesus.

John 3:16 is very clear that *God so loved the world that He gave His one and only Son, so that everyone who believes in Him will not perish but have eternal life!*

Everyone. Anyone. That's *me* . . . that's *YOU!*

His is an invitation open to EVERYONE!

But in order to know just how good *that* news is, you have to be aware of some bad news as well . . .

The bad news is that all of us, myself included, are born sinners—who screw life up a lot more often than we get it right.

Romans 3:23 says that *everyone has sinned; we all fall short of God's glorious standard* (of perfection).

Again, that's everyone! ALL of us. No exceptions.

There's nothing any of us can do on our own can to make ourselves *better* (much less *worthy)!* Absolutely nothing!

It is only by the shed blood of Jesus that any of us are ever perfected. It's by acknowledging all our screw-ups and saying: "Jesus, I believe in You! Only You can make all this better; only You can make me *well!*"

Only then are we made *new.*

You see, He isn't some "out there" God, orchestrating things from a safe (but aloof) distance. He is living and active and as close to you right now as the mention of His Name. He speaks directly to your heart through His Spirit and, if you'll just open yourself up to Him, He'll do that *forever!*

We hear a lot of talk about religion and spirituality, and most of us try to take a little bit of this and a little bit of that 'til we come up with something that fits us or find something that seems to work for us. Problem is: that's not the way it works!

The Bible is clear that there is only ONE way to Heaven (and eternal life) and that passes directly through Jesus Christ!

You wanna know what I really love about God?

I love the fact that the Creator of the Universe is also my very best Friend!

I love the fact that, while He cares about the *multitudes,* He also loves *ME*—a lot more than I do, in fact!

Truth is—He's crazy about me . . . and He's crazy about *YOU* too!

Even while He's busy sorting out the problems in Washington or the Middle East, He's never too busy for you! He really wants to speak to you and hear from you. I love that!

Maybe you need to take a step of faith and embrace Jesus for yourself. If you've never done so, then I promise you that's your greatest and most pressing need!

Or maybe you did that a long time ago, but have gotten off-track and really need Him to help correct your course!

Either way, this is YOUR opportunity to do just that!

Maybe you got more than you bargained for when you picked up this book. You were just looking forward to laughing and learning some "Lessons from a Loser."

But I'd be doing you a grave disservice if I didn't leave you with the one lesson that matters most.

If what you're reading is resonating and the little hairs on the back of your neck are standing up right now, that's the Spirit of God—Who's inviting you into a personal relationship with Him!

Whatever you have (or haven't) thought about or done with Jesus in the past, would you just STOP right now and, right where you are, say this prayer along with me:

Father –

*I know that I'm a sinner and a screw-up—
but You died on the cross for me to make me well
and, because You didn't stay dead, I believe You really can
do that—
and I love You for all of that!
I claim You as my Savior, and from this moment on
(with Your help),
I'll call You my Lord!
In Jesus' Name, I embrace You!
With all of my heart, I embrace You!*

Amen!

If you just made that the prayer of your heart, then let me be the first to welcome you to the family! I celebrate that decision with you!

I can tell you from my own experience that this doesn't mean that, from this point on, life is always going to be easy. It simply means that now you'll have somewhere to turn (and Someone to turn to) when it gets hard!

Thank you for taking this journey with me. I trust the Lord will use these 44 lessons in your life as He has in mine—as you discover the very specific (and unspeakably wonderful) plan and purpose He has mapped out for YOU!

He really loves you! And so do I.

ENDNOTES

1. Mark Batterson, *Draw the Circle* (Grand Rapids, MI: Zondervan, 2012), p. 27.

2. Copyright © 1981, 1982, by Charles R. Swindoll, Inc. All rights reserved worldwide. Used by permission. www.insight.org.

FREQUENTLY ASKED QUESTIONS

I've noticed that, ever since coming off the show, I get many of the same questions (over and over again) everywhere I go. Because many of YOU probably have these same questions, I thought I'd address a few of them here. In no particular order, here are the Top 10 questions that I am most frequently asked . . .

1. How did you become a contestant on *The Biggest Loser*?

I have loved *The Biggest Loser* from the time it premiered in 2004. As I mentioned in Chapter 14, I actually wrote a Facebook post back in 2009 confessing my secret desire to be a contestant on the show someday.

Five years later, when I saw their Facebook post (in March of 2014) encouraging former athletes to fill out an application, I jumped at the chance! Once I sent the application off, however, I forgot all about it . . . until I received an e-mail (about four weeks later) inviting me to an Open Casting Call at *The Biggest Loser* Resort in Itasca, Illinois!

I was one of about 1,000 people there that day. They brought us in (in groups of about 20 at a time) and gave us exactly three minutes to share our stories. As we were on our way out, they said: "If you don't hear from us by 10 P.M. tonight, then it's a 'no-go'."

Thinking that had been the biggest waste of a reasonably good Saturday, I peeled out of the parking lot in search of a Portillo's hot dog! (Hey—don't judge me! I was trying out for *The Biggest Loser*, not *The Bachelorette*—and this girl wanted a hot dog!) I'd no sooner bitten into my hot dog when my cellphone rang. Someone from *The Biggest Loser* wanted to know if I would come back the following Tuesday for a 20-minute, one-on-one interview in downtown Chicago! Hello?! You didn't have to ask ME twice!

My 20-minute interview that next Tuesday turned into two hours—which is when I began to believe that this might actually happen! "Sonya," I said to myself, "you'd better fasten your seat belt . . . 'cuz you could be in for the ride of your life!"

After I shot and submitted the requested audition video, I didn't hear a thing for another six weeks. Then, all of a sudden, the requests started pouring in. Photos, contracts, one piece of information after another . . . I complied with their every request until, finally (one day in May), I got the call saying: "Pack your bags! You're coming to LA for casting finals!"

On June 9, 2014 (as detailed in Chapter One)—I boarded a plane from Springfield, Illinois to Los Angeles, California . . . not knowing if I was leaving for five *days* or five *months*. Upon landing in LA, I went into nearly two weeks of casting finals . . . before moving onto the Ranch (as an official contestant).

2. What was a typical "day in the life" while on the show?

Quite frankly, there wasn't a typical day—but four different *types* of days.

On a *dark* day, we were left to work out on our own—with no cameras present.

I would typically begin a dark day with my 6:44 AM "prayer walk" around the Ranch, before moving into my first fitness routine of the day, lasting exactly 88 (44 x 2) minutes. I would then eat breakfast and, after letting my food digest for precisely 44 minutes, would start my routine all over again (repeating this process five to six times a day).

My fitness routines varied, depending on what Jen prescribed for us, but always included a lot of cardio. Even on dark days, Jen (alone among the trainers) was often at the Ranch working out with us (yet another reason our White Team was so strong, in my opinion).

Dark days were my favorite—because they offered not only the greatest calorie burns but the time and opportunity to really talk to each other.

On a *filming* day, the routine was much the same . . . except for the fact that we spent much of our time on-camera. We had to be dressed in our *Biggest Loser* gear, and at least one of our several workouts that day would be filmed (along with multiple interviews). It could be difficult to work out when on-camera and, on filming days, the cameras were usually rolling for 10-12 hours a day! In spite of the challenges, filming was actually a lot of fun, and you eventually forgot that the cameras were even there.

My least favorite was the *challenge* day. We started off with Sand Mountain and, from that point forward, I really dreaded challenge days! In fact, I often struggled with anxiety—since there was no way to know just how difficult the next challenge would be!

We generally tried to avoid any strenuous workout *before* the challenges because we never knew what type of "hurting" would be put on us and how much energy it would require!

If there was one day that we dreaded even more, however, it was the *weigh-in* day . . . which was guaranteed to end badly—since someone would be going home! Even if it was not You, your relief would be mixed with the sadness of losing a friend whom you'd grown to love and respect.

Weigh-in days inevitably got off to an early start (with everyone having to pee in a cup . . . to make sure both that we were hydrated and NOT using any weight-loss drugs) and meant long hours on-camera in the gym and doing interviews.

3. Did you have a chef preparing your meals while you were on the show?

No such luck! We were responsible for preparing all of our own meals. We did, however, have a wonderful dietitian (Cheryl Forberg) at our disposal. While she wasn't actually in residence on the Ranch, she met with us regularly, counseled us from afar, and was always readily available to us (via phone call or Skype).

Our refrigerators, freezers, and pantries were kept fully stocked with fresh, healthy foods. Not all of it was organic, but there was never any shortage of whole food (not heavily processed or refined).

We also had a library of *Biggest Loser* cookbooks at our fingertips, but we were in charge of making our own meals. In the end, that proved to be great preparation for coming home!

4. What was the BEST thing about being on *The Biggest Loser*?

That one is easy: the *relationships!* In a very short period of time, I was able to build deep and meaningful relationships with my trainer, team, castmates, and all of the crew who worked on the show. I grew to love each one dearly—and miss them every day (to this day)! Losing weight was great, but adding friends and building relationships is what really made our time on the show golden.

5. Was it easier to *lose* the weight or to *keep* it off?

No doubt about it—*losing* the weight was a piece of cake (no pun intended) compared to *keeping* it off!

Don't misunderstand me—working out and learning to eat correctly (while on the show) was plenty hard. The workouts were often brutal, and there were days when I wasn't at all sure I was even going to make it through! I worked harder to *lose* those 144 pounds than I ever had anything in my life!

That said, *keeping* the weight off since I've been home has proven to be my most difficult battle, by far!

Home, after all, is where I'm surrounded by everything (work, daily responsibilities, difficult people, etc.) that helped me become morbidly obese in the first place! Let's face it: everyday life can be unbelievably stressful at times!

While on the show, it was easy for me (particularly as an athlete in the throes of competition) to stay laser-focused on the one and only task with which I needed to concern myself: losing weight. *Since* the show, however, building a healthy relationship with food and exercise has been very difficult. It's a constant battle . . . but one I intend to keep on winning.

6. What's the key to *keeping* your weight off?

It's actually a pretty basic formula: *diet* and *exercise!*

Of course, sticking to either requires a lot of hard work and dedication—but there is simply no substitute for good, old-fashioned diet and exercise.

Just to be clear, I'm not talking about any specific diet— just your normal, daily food regimen. And while I firmly believe that exercise is important, for me personally, diet plays a much greater role.

Either way, there is no magic pill, potion, or shake. You simply have to start taking in less and moving a little more! In my experience, I have found that, so long as I eat correctly, the weight will stay off.

Here are some things that work for me:

- I stay away from a processed foods as much as possible.

- I try to eat a lot of one-ingredient foods. Not one-*word* foods (like pizza), but one-*ingredient* foods: beef, chicken, fish, apple, orange, carrot, spinach, oatmeal, quinoa . . . you get the picture.

- I seldom go to a restaurant without first checking out the menu online and deciding what I'm going to order before I ever walk in the door.

If you're addicted to food (or anything else, for that matter), then you HAVE to have a game plan in order to succeed! I wasn't the first to say it but, as I continue to tell people all the time: "If you fail to plan, then you plan to fail!" If you are going to be successful, then you have to develop a game plan and stick to it!

But, for everyone I know, both diet *and* exercise are key to long-term success.

7. Besides diet and exercise, what *else* is important in long-term weight loss?

While I firmly believe that diet and exercise are key, for me personally, there are two *additional* things that played an even more significant role . . .

1. Counseling (to understand my battle with emotional eating)

2. My relationship with Jesus

I dedicated three entire chapters in this book to my counseling journey—in hopes of helping you recognize just how critically important it is to gain an understanding of your relationship with food. You always know *what* you eat . . . but you may not know *why* you eat it! Once you're armed with *that* information, it becomes a little easier to make wiser choices and decisions that are based on *fact,* not *emotion.*

For me personally, however, the most critical factor of all is my relationship with Jesus! If my relationship with Him is strong, then I am typically unshakable. I believe what God says in His Word when He promises to fight the battle for me (sometimes by giving *me* the strength to win) . . .

"Don't be afraid; the Lord your God Himself will fight for you" (Deuteronomy 3:22).

"What then shall we say to these things? If God is for us, who can be against us?" (Romans 8:31).

"Be strong and courageous. Do not be afraid; do not be discouraged, for the Lord your God will be with you wherever you go" (Joshua 1:9).

And one of my personal favorites: *"I can do everything through Christ Who gives me strength"* (Philippians 4:13 - NLT).

I've found that when I submit the battle to Him, He will fight it for me!

8. How did being a Christ-follower impact you while on *The Biggest Loser* Ranch?

In every possible way. In my relationships, in the way I treated people, in my work ethic . . . Being a Christ-follower has nothing to do with where you live or the circumstances in which you find yourself at any given moment. Being a Christ-follower simply means doing your best to follow Him every step of the way every moment of the day . . . in every decision you make (both great and small).

Being a follower of Christ allowed me to weather everything that came my way while on the show. I had complete peace that I would be there for the perfect amount of time. God knew exactly how long He wanted me there—and I realized that, if I can trust Him in the little things, then I can trust Him in the big things too!

I want my life to be a light for the Gospel of Jesus Christ, and that affects every decision that I make. I certainly don't always get it right . . . but I hope that my actions will continuously pull others closer to Christ rather than drive them away.

9. You mention your faith a lot. What do you do to deepen your walk with the Lord?

I'm not sure there's a perfect formula. With time and experimentation, however, I've found some things that help me experience a vibrant and ever-present relationship with a never-changing God.

These are some of the things that I do most consistently:

- I read my Bible every single day. It's the living and active Word of God that is my standard for faith and conduct. It's the primary way that God speaks to me.

- I pray every single day—many times a day. I don't mean that I set aside two hours of uninterrupted prayer time or anything like that. I just talk to Him consistently all throughout the day: while I'm still lying in bed in the morning, in the shower getting ready for the day, in my car on the way to work, on the job and in meetings—in other words, anywhere and everywhere! I also try to listen carefully to whatever He may be speaking to my heart and then act on it.

- I'm active in a local church. God tells us (in Hebrews 10:25) not to forsake the regular gathering of believers, so I think that's important.

- I'm actively involved in ministry (choir, in my case) at my local church to help build up the body to go out and impact the world!

- I listen to a lot of great pastors online. There are many terrific pastors sharing God's Word in some remarkable ways. Among my favorites are Craig Groeschel (Life Church), Steven Furtick (Elevation), and Andy Stanley (North Point Community Church), to name just a few.

- I like to journal—which allows me to see and remember more readily Who God is and how He's working in my life.

- I have set up a "War Room" in my home—where I go to spend concentrated time alone with God as I seek His face and allow Him to equip me for the spiritual battles raging all around me.

- I love listening to worship music around the house and in my car. For me, it's a wonderful way to fix my focus on the greatness of God.

Everyone is different, of course—but I encourage you to find those things that will draw YOU closer to the heart of the One Who made you . . . and for Whom you were made!

10. If you had to do it over, would you still go on *The Biggest Loser*?

YES—in a heartbeat! I had a phenomenal experience on the Ranch. I thoroughly loved all the people involved—and always felt loved, cared for, and respected in return. For that reason, I tell people all the time that I would gladly leave home tomorrow to go do it all over again. It was nothing short of amazing—and I will be eternally grateful to have had this opportunity.

ACKNOWLEDGMENTS

There are so many people I want to thank—without whom this book would never have become a reality . . .

- Jesus – Without You, I am nothing; with You, I am everything. Thank You for loving me enough to die for me. Thank You for Your love, faithfulness, mercy, and grace. I want nothing more than to honor You with my words and my life. I give my whole heart and life to You, my Lord and my God.

- Christopher Burcham – My co-author and my friend. A simple "thank you" doesn't even begin to express how much I appreciate you. You have taken my jumbled stories and thoughts and turned them into a beautiful offering that we can share with the world. I have asked God repeatedly to give your time and resources back to you tenfold. I'm also deeply grateful to your amazing and beautiful wife Amanda for her support of this entire venture. Thank you. I love you both.

- Mom and Dad – Your support throughout my entire life has been nothing short of astounding. Thank you for making me the unique "Redneck Asian" that I am today – and for showing me the value of hard work and perseverance. I thank God for giving me such amazing parents and I will be forever grateful for your love and support.

- My Jones-A-Palooza Girls – Thank you for loving me even when I'm at my most unlovable. I am so grateful for your ability to see beyond my mess and forgive and love me still. I love you girls so much and thank God for you everyday.

- All the *rest* of my family – aunts, uncles, and cousins near and far. Thank you for always loving and supporting me. Special thanks to my crazy Uncle Bob, who has always been one of my biggest fans – but is also a true testament of what it means to love and serve God with your whole heart. You are a truly amazing man, Uncle Bob – and I am honored to be your niece.

- Jeni Phelps – You have been both my roommate and my best friend for nearly 20 years. I am so grateful that God caused our paths to cross back in 1999 (and that you chose not to listen to your first instincts about me being a lunatic). It has truly been an honor to do life with you and I love you more than I can say. Thanks for always believing in me and making me better. God has gifted you in so many ways . . . thank you for using those gifts to draw others closer to the cross of Christ. You're an amazing woman, Jeni!

- Steve, Carolyn, and Jaci Phelps – Thank you for being my extended family for nearly 20 years! I love you all.

- My Girls – Jeni Phelps, Donita Schrey, Tina Casper, Sheiler Hohimer, LaDonna Smith, Brittany Wallin, Aubrey Emerson, Kendra Bryse, Kim Luz, Jenna Luz – each of you make my life so much better and I love doing life with you. Thank you for showing me that life is always better when you share it with amazing people, helping me not to take myself too seriously, and for always encouraging me to love Jesus more than anything else. I love you all!

- Julie Tucker-Ponder – You started out as my counselor but have since become a wonderful colleague and friend. Thank you for seeing beyond all the yuck and hurt that I didn't even want to talk about and showing me the beauty of what's inside of me. Thank you for being kind, patient, and for seeing the very best in me even when I couldn't see it for myself. I honestly believe that you are the very BEST counselor for people who are battling eating disorders! You've helped so many people (myself included) and I'm beyond grateful to God for you. I love you, my friend. (To anyone in the Springfield, Illinois area struggling with an eating disorder, I urge you to contact Julie Tucker-Ponder at Psychiatric

Associates of Central Illinois. Trust me—you'll be glad you did!)

- Gavin Gardner– Thanks for all the time that you took to help me create my audition video for *The Biggest Loser*. You (and all the Gardners—Katie, Tyler, and Griffin) are absolutely awesome! Hope you all get to have Snacks Er'Day. Love you.

- Williamsville/Sherman Community Unit School District staff, students, and families – I cannot even begin to tell you how grateful I am for the support that you gave me during my time on the show. I was lucky to be able to share my experience with YOU! You helped make my run on *The Biggest Loser* a tremendous experience for me; I can't thank you enough. And Dave Root . . . thank you, my friend. Your legacy continues to live on through the amazing people in the WCUSD 15 School District. Thanks for your example. (P.S. If you cut me, I still bleed purple and gold!)

- Tammie Rue – You're more than my *friend;* you're my *sister*—and I love you. You've been a pretty great running buddy and accountability partner too, and I am beyond grateful for all your support!

- My SES Prayer Group Girls – Liz Huebner, Amy Kluemke, Kathy Scheffler, and Carissa Szoke (in addition to the aforementioned Tammie) – the friendship, praises, and prayer requests that we've shared for so many years remain the source of some of my fondest memories. I love you.

- COTFDP – Mindy Ashbaugh and Matt Mead – We started out at fellow coaches and ended up the best of friends. I could never have anticipated the impact that the two of you would have in my life. You didn't just make me a better *coach;* you made me a better *person.* I love you both dearly and will be forever grateful for your friendship. Mindy . . . that hug the night of Finale . . . couldn't have shared that with anyone else but YOU. Love you!

- Jen Widerstrom – This goes beyond this. Truly. Always has, always will. Thank you for believing in me when I didn't!

- My fellow members of the White Team – Rondalee Beardsley, Woody Carter, Toma Dobrosavljevic, Matt Miller, and JJ O'Malley (in addition to Jen herself, of course). We started as strangers, became teammates, turned into friends, and eventually became family. You pushed me, encouraged me, loved me, laughed—and cried—with me! You are each a huge part of my heart and will remain so forever.

- Lori Mack– My "Eeyore" – You truly are stronger than you know and better than you believe. I love you.

- Cheryl Forberg – Thank you for your continued and consistent friendship—even beyond the Ranch. Love you so much, beautiful lady!

- *Biggest Loser* Season 16 contestants, trainers, and production team – I cannot begin to put into words just how much you all mean to me. Thanks for taking a chance on me . . . and for loving me so well. I love you right back!

- A special shout-out to some others on *The Biggest Loser* who always went out of their way to take really great care of us: Kelly Hudson, Alisha Pennington, and Smadar Bezalel . . . we couldn't have asked for a better athletic training staff. You girls were the best (even though you incessantly lied to us all season long). Joel Relampagos, Kat Elmore, Kasey Bates, Kristen "Mearnsey" Hogan, Ryan Sommer, and countless others . . . thanks for all your love and care. You guys are amazing!

- Melinda Clark, Dr. Loren Hughes, Vince Noel, Craig Brace, and team at HSHS Medical Group – Thank you for making one of my biggest dreams come true—by giving me the opportunity of a lifetime to partner with you in positively impacting the lives of people in Central and Southern Illinois. What an honor it is to work alongside you as we carry forth the vision that the Sisters had so many years ago. It's an honor to work for HSHS Medical Group.

- Whitney Canterbury– You made the book; now hush! You're awesome.

- Kary Oberbrunner and Author Academy Elite Tribe – Thank you for holding my hand every step of the way during this book process. I appreciate you so much.

- Greenville University – You have helped make me what I am today. Thanks for discipling me when I was just a young 'un! Lori Gaffner . . . you're the best mentor I've ever known! I love you! Thanks for your investment in me.

- Calvary Church Family – Thanks for consistently encouraging me to follow hard after Jesus.

- Dan and Glynnis Shryock – The greatest couple that I know – I love you both more than I can say.

- Why Not You Today Conference Team – YOU! I LOVE YOU! Thank you ALL for your dedication to making the Why Not You Today Conference be tremendous days of impact for women.

- Polly Parsons at Apt. C Photography in Springfield, Illinois – Your work (which is all throughout this book) is absolutely brilliant and I cannot thank you enough for the beautiful shots you took. I so appreciate your time and your friendship!

- Jan Brandenburg and April Jones - Thank you for your hours of proofing, editing, comments, and suggestions! Most importantly, thank you for your friendship. I love you both.

- Rocky – My favorite 74-pound pit bull who is the current love of my life. I love the unconditional love that you bring.

- People in the book – All of you in this book helped make the stories great (and the reality greater)! I honor and thank you for your impact in my life.

Granny Betty Milnes - You truly were the most magnificent 100-year-old woman I've ever known (and one of the most beautiful women in the world)! I only wish this could have been completed in time for you to see it. I love you and I'll miss waving to you from the choir. You fought the good fight.

ABOUT THE AUTHORS

Sonya Jones captured the hearts of viewers with her upbeat attitude and dedication to succeed on Season 16 of NBC's reality TV show *The Biggest Loser*. Jones was that season's only female finalist—with the closest margin of loss in *Biggest Loser* history (.01% of her body weight).

Knowing that, as a physical education teacher, she should be the model of health and fitness, Jones felt like a hypocrite as she neared 300 pounds in 2014. Six months later, she stepped onto the scale (and into the hearts of millions of Americans)—dropping a whopping 144 pounds to lose 50.88% of her total body weight on national television.

Prior to her *Biggest Loser* journey, Jones earned a degree in Physical Education from Greenville University (in Greenville, Illinois—where she was inducted into the Athletic Hall of Fame in 2018) along with graduate degrees in Educational Leadership and Administration from the University of Illinois at Springfield.

A former semi-professional athlete (two-time Collegiate All-American in fastpitch softball), Jones spent nearly two decades in education before taking her current position as an Outreach Representative for HSHS Medical Group in central Illinois. She is a certified (and widely-sought) speaker with the John Maxwell Team. When not engaged in public speaking all over the country—she enjoys playing softball, spending quality time with friends and family, and pursuing her most recent interest: rescuing pit bulls.

Christopher Burcham, and I could not be any more different, but together, we make a pretty good team!

Christopher E. Burcham may be small in stature himself, but is privileged to spend his life proclaiming a God about Whom *nothing* is small!

After graduating from Bryan College (in Dayton, Tennessee) with a degree in Biblical Studies and doing graduate work in Christian Ministries at Huntington University (in Huntington, Indiana), Burcham has spent the past 28 years in vocational ministry—both as a pastor and classroom teacher in Illinois, Florida, and North Carolina. He is currently in his 11th year of service as the Senior Pastor of Union Hill Baptist Church in Clemmons, North Carolina.

Burcham is joined in life and ministry by his lovely wife Amanda—who was raised Mormon, dabbled in witchcraft, and eventually become a flaming agnostic before being radically saved and going on to serve as a missionary (with YWAM Int'l) in Hawaii, China, and Tibet—prior to becoming a pastor's wife.

Burcham is an avid history buff who has been privileged to meet the last nine U. S. presidents (from Richard Nixon through Donald Trump)—all in connection with a book he is currently writing, entitled: *Heads of State; Feet of Clay.*

With my co-author, Christopher Burcham
and his lovely wife Amanda

Thanks to Polly Parsons at Apt. C Photography
for some really great shots

A "Why Not You Today" Conference

Spirit lead me
where my trust is without borders
Let me walk upon the waters
Wherever You would call me
Take me deeper than my feet could ever wander
And my faith will be made stronger
In the presence of my Savior

Pray like it all depends on God . . . because it DOES!

BOOK SONYA TO SPEAK
AT YOUR EVENT!

Sonya's communication style will have you crying tears of laughter and joy while also tugging at your heartstrings as she empowers you to fall in love with your life and yourself. As a former coach by profession, it is one of Sonya's goals in life to help you believe that you can accomplish more than you ever hoped, dreamed, or imagined! Not only will she give you the tools to succeed, she will also give you the belief that you can succeed. Through her personal experience of shedding the weight physically, but growing in every other area of her life, she will inspire to you be the best version of you that you can be.

Sonya is an Independent Certified Coach, Teacher and Speaker with The John Maxwell Team.

SONYAJONES44.COM

WHY NOT
YOU
TODAY

WOMEN'S CONFERENCE

A WOMEN'S CONFERENCE WITH SONYA JONES & FRIENDS THAT WILL MOTIVATE, INSPIRE, AND ENCOURAGE YOU TO BE THE BEST VERSION OF YOU THAT YOU CAN BE!

Bring this event to your town!
VISIT SONYAJONES44.COM FOR MORE INFO

CPSIA information can be obtained
at www.ICGtesting.com
Printed in the USA
LVHW04*0551071018
592660LV00001B/1/P